SESSIONS WITH ISAIAH

Smyth & Helwys Publishing, Inc.
6316 Peake Road
Macon, Georgia 31210-3960
1-800-747-3016
© 2017 by James M. King

Library of Congress Cataloging-in-Publication Data

Names: King, James Mattison, 1951- author.
Title: Sessions with Isaiah : what to do when the world caves in / by James
M. King.
Description: Macon : Smyth & Helwys, 2017. | Includes bibliographical
references.
Identifiers: LCCN 2017002603 | ISBN 9781573129428 (pbk. : alk. paper)
Subjects: LCSH: Bible. Isaiah--Criticism, interpretation, etc. |
Suffering--Biblical teaching. | Consolation--Biblical teaching.
Classification: LCC BS1515.6.S8 K56 2017 | DDC 224/.107--dc23
LC record available at https://lccn.loc.gov/2017002603

Sessions *with* Isaiah

● ● ● *What to Do* When the *World Caves In*

James M. King

SMYTH&HELWYS
PUBLISHING, INCORPORATED ▪ MACON, GEORGIA

For Hattie, Rudy, and Iris,
three grandchildren of promise born
after this manuscript was completed

Contents

Introducing Isaiah

When the world is about to cave in, what happens next? When you have exhausted all your resources and there seems to be nowhere to turn, what do you do? These questions are as old as humanity, and we all face them at one time or another. The questions may arise as a result of circumstances beyond our control: the devastating diagnosis of an illness, the death of a spouse, abandonment by a close relation, or the loss of a job. It is just as likely that we consider such questions because we are facing the consequences of our actions: the revelation of misconduct leads to the loss of reputation, profligate spending or gambling results in financial ruin, willfully poor performance on the job ends in termination, or unfaithfulness causes the loss of a spouse or family.

Regardless of the reasons behind a person's desperate circumstances, the natural, almost universal human response is a frantic cry of distress: *What do I do now?* And when whole groups or even nations confront such circumstances, the inherent questions remain the same. *What do we do now?*

How do believers face such crises from a spiritual perspective? How does an individual, a people, or a nation respond spiritually to great stress? Some abandon faith in a higher power. *If there is a God, why does that God allow such terrible things to happen to me?* People who cannot deny the existence of God still question God's concern with their lives. *A divine being may have set things in motion, but clearly that being has no interest in me.* Some seek the solace and protection of the gods of the conquerors. *I prayed to my God, and he failed me. I'm going to try some other object of faith.* Others cling to the hope that a deliverer will come. *I need someone to show me who God is.* And still others are so painfully aware of the depth of their sin that they see no reason to expect divine assistance. *I'm in too deep. I could never be good enough for God.*

In the time of national deterioration and humiliation and suffering that began more than seven hundred years before the Common Era, the members of the covenantal people known as the children of Israel or the people of Judah had all these responses.

Following the death of King Solomon, Israel was divided into two separate kingdoms. The southern kingdom comprised the tribes of Judah and Benjamin and much of the tribe of Levi. This kingdom was subsequently referred to as Judah. The northern kingdom of Israel comprised the remaining ten tribes.

The northern kingdom was taken into captivity by the Assyrians in the eighth century BCE. Through successive invasions and deportations, they were settled in "the cities of the Medes" (2 Kgs 15:29).

It is the southern kingdom, known as Judah, to whom the original Isaiah prophesied. It will be this nation, less than one hundred fifty years later, that will fall to the Babylonian Empire. In the time of national deterioration and humiliation and suffering that began over seven hundred years before the Common Era, the people of Judah asked these questions about what to do when one's world caves in.

During this dark period in Israel's history, the southern kingdom began to decline in power, and its deterioration continued through the Babylonian captivity of a large portion of the people and their eventual return to the land of Israel beginning around 540 BCE (Before the Common Era). Idolatry, reliance on foreign powers, failure to care for the poor among them, insincere worship, and many other evils—all despite the warnings of God's faithful spokesmen—eventually led to national disgrace and finally to captivity. After ignoring warnings and suffering the consequences, the question for Israel during this period came down to this: *When the world caves in, what then?*

For the people of Judah, captivity meant more than forced removal to a new and oppressive location. It was a dislocation from the Land of Promise. The city of Jerusalem and the surrounding countryside was sacred ground, given to their ancestors by Yahweh and evidence that God was blessing them. To live in Babylon was to be exiled both geographically and theologically. They were being exiled from their homes, but also, as they interpreted it in their despair, from the presence of God.

Through this period, individuals stood as bridges between the people and their God. Some tried to warn of the actions that would lead the people to desperation. Others sought to provide comfort once sin had resulted in punishment. Still others offered God's instruction for how the nation should conduct itself once a relationship with God and with the land of promise had been restored. These were the prophets who heard clear and pointed messages from Yahweh and delivered them to the chosen people. They were there to answer, on God's behalf, the natural question of all who find themselves in dire straits: *What do we do now?*

The book we find in Hebrew Scripture (the Christian Old Testament) known as Isaiah covers this entire period. It begins in the years of national stress when, under various kings, Israel was surrounded by more powerful neighbors and foolishly sought foreign alliances rather than dependence on Yahweh. It continues when the natural result of that unfaithfulness was conquest by the great power in the region, Babylon, and the captivity of many of the best and brightest in that foreign land. The book concludes with anticipation of return to the land of promise and strong admonitions about how the people's conduct should be reformed, lest their punishment be even worse.

Christians of every era have found this sacred text to be of great value in understanding their relationship to God and in seeing Israel's relationship with Yahweh as a prototype for the church's relationship with God as revealed in Jesus Christ. Indeed, when seeking to understand the connection between the God of Abraham, Isaac, and Jacob and the God made flesh in the historical figure of Jesus, the writers of the New Testament relied on the words of Isaiah more than those of any other prophet.

Christians who wish to study this complex and wide-ranging book devotionally should understand two essential concepts: the historical situation and how the Hebrews understood their relationship with God. In the pages of Isaiah's sixty-six chapters, we not only find stern warnings against the kinds of behavior that distance us from God but also hear the incredibly reassuring messages of comfort and restoration that are offered to all who repent.

Through it all, there is the promise of a Deliverer, one who comes not as a conquering political or military hero, but as a Suffering Servant, Wonderful Counselor, Mighty God, Everlasting Father, and Prince of Peace. We cannot fully grasp the nature of those terms as applied to Jesus until we see them foretold in the life of Israel as depicted in the book of Isaiah. Take the time to delve into this rich and relevant ancient book.

Structure of Isaiah

Biblical scholars have long recognized that, though the Book of Isaiah appears in both the Hebrew Scriptures and the Christian canon as a single work, it is the product of more than one author and covers at least two, and probably three, periods of history.

The first thirty-nine chapters of Isaiah are closely related to the events that occurred in the Middle East of the latter half of the eighth century BCE. The prophet begins his account by reciting the kings of Judah who reigned during that time. The first twelve chapters are addressed to Judah. Chapters 13–27 are a series of warnings and promises to the nations that surround Judah, and chapters 28–39 return to Judah once again. Chapters 36–39 are a duplication of material found in 2 Kings 18 and following. In this first major section of the book, the prophet details the crisis brought about by the rise of the Assyrian Empire and warns about the danger of foreign alliances, but there is no evidence that the original prophet whom we know as Isaiah continued to prophesy after 701 BCE.

There is a very clear change at the beginning of chapter 40. Now the location is Babylon, and as such can be dated from the destruction of Jerusalem in 587 BCE, some 150 years after the death of the original prophet Isaiah. As we will see in more detail later, this marks the period when a large portion of the people of Judah were forcibly removed from the Land of Promise and carried into Babylon. Because this large group of Israelites are in exile, away from home, and oppressed, the tone of the prophecies is completely different from that of the first section of the book. Here the message is of encouragement during severe crisis and a promise that they will be set free and allowed to return home.

The third section of the book may be slightly later still. Chapters 56–66 are more poetic and appear to be from the early days of return to the land when the people are trying to rebuild the city of Jerusalem.

This interpretation of the structure of Isaiah in no way argues against its divine inspiration but only addresses the contexts in which it was written and the most likely divisions of the material we know today as the Book of Isaiah.

A Courageous Prophet

The book begins with the oracles of a prophet of Yahweh who bears the name Isaiah, which means "The Lord is salvation." Reading back through the mists of time and history, it is impossible for us to know how much of what has become the canonical book of Isaiah is connected to a single individual by that name. Most modern scholars have concluded that the material from chapters 40 through 66 belongs to either an exilic or postexilic period that would have been beyond the lifespan of the original prophet.

Also, there is considerable internal evidence that most of the first thirty-nine chapters have been edited, amended, and added to so that their result is more of a reinterpretation and application of the oracles of Isaiah than a transcription of what he prophesied in the eighth century BCE. In the eighth chapter of Isaiah there is a reference to disciples of Isaiah (Isa 8:16-22). These disciples were probably the ones who maintained and possibly edited the writings that have come to us as the first thirty-nine chapters of the book. There is a tradition that Isaiah was cut to pieces during the religious persecutions during the reign of Manasseh, the pro-Assyrian king who followed Hezekiah as monarch in Judah (Kelley, 150).

Almost nothing regarding the personal life of the prophet can be said with certainty. The first verse of the oracle tells us that his father's name was Amoz. Judging from the internal evidence regarding the reigns of kings over Judah, Isaiah was born between 770 and 760 BCE. This means he would have been between twenty and thirty years of age when he began to prophesy. Dating his ministry by the reigns of the kings under whose leadership he serves (Isa 1:1), he probably prophesied for at least forty years. At the end of the thirty-ninth chapter, when King Hezekiah rejects Isaiah's warning regarding an alliance with Assyria, Isaiah withdraws from public life.

The first verse of the book of Isaiah lets us know that the prophet was active during the reigns of Uzziah, Jotham, Ahaz, and Hezekiah, kings of Judah. According to Isaiah's account of his calling to prophetic ministry in chapter 6, he began his career in the year of Uzziah's death, which would have been somewhere around 740 BCE. The last historical event on which he comments is the fall of Jerusalem, which took place in 701. However, if the account of the kings during whose reigns he lived is correct, his observations of the history of Judah and the nation's relationship with their God may have lasted for over sixty years.

Nevertheless, enough biographical information appears in those first thirty-nine chapters to let us know that there was an individual who received a message from God for the people of Judah, who courageously spoke that word to both kings and commoners, and who was thoroughly involved in the historic events that led to the demise of the southern kingdom and the period of the exile. He was married, and his wife is called a "prophetess," but that may have simply meant that she was married to a prophet. They had two sons, and Isaiah gave them names (as we will see later) that provide commentary on historical events of the time.

Their first son was Shear-jashub (7:3), which means "A remnant shall return." Because this birth appears to have taken place early in the chronology of the book, being placed in the chapter immediately following the account of Isaiah's call to prophesy, it would appear to be an early note of hope before the more than two centuries of devastation in Judah. Each time the prophet called the name of his eldest son, it would have been a reminder that, after years of punishment and deprivation, some of the people of Judah would one day be returned to their land.

The name of Isaiah's second son at first appears less hopeful. It is Maher-shalal-hash-baz (8:3), which means "Swift to come is the spoil, speedy is the prey." The name is the same as an inscription Isaiah had been instructed by God to write on a large tablet in public view, although at the time no one would have understood the events to which it referred. To the initial viewers it might have appeared to be a warning about the fate of the southern kingdom of Judah. The child's conception and birth came at a time when King Ahaz and the people of Judah were threatened by Syria and Israel. However, God explained to Isaiah that "before the child knows how to call 'My father' or 'My mother,' the wealth of Damascus and the spoil of Samaria will be carried away by the king of Assyria" (8:4). Instead of being about Judah, the "prey" refers to their enemies. Although Judah appeared to be imperiled by these two kingdoms, the perceived threat would never become reality.

The names of Isaiah's sons were chosen by Yahweh. Not only by speaking through Isaiah but also by involving Isaiah's sons, God sent messages to the people of Judah. The choice for the name of the second son dealt with events in Isaiah's own time, while that of the first offered hope for a future almost two centuries distant.

The Character of the Prophet

In the classic work *The Message of the Prophets,* Gerhard von Rad says that "The preaching of Isaiah represents the theological high-water mark of the whole Old Testament." He believed that "Not one of the other prophets approaches Isaiah in intellectual vigor or, more particularly, in the magnificent sweep of his ideas" (118).

The characteristic that von Rad most closely identified with Isaiah was *moderation*, a restraint in the face of great sin, crisis, and political uncertainty. After his encounter with the holiness of God recorded in the sixth chapter, Isaiah carried to the people a message of outrage regarding their conduct. This message was always tempered, however, by the promise of hope, if not for his hearers, then at least for the faithful remnant who would survive.

Harking back to the contingent covenant on which their relationship with Yahweh was always based, there is the promise of redemption and prosperity. However, if the people rebel, their destruction will soon be at hand. The choice is theirs. This is consistently the message throughout the first thirty-nine chapters of the book, the section identified with the original prophet.

Even the narrative of Isaiah's call, wherein the details of his commissioning include the troubling news that his preaching will make the minds of the people dull, concludes with the hopeful, enigmatic words relating to the image of Judah as a burned-out tree, "The holy seed is its stump" (Isa 6:13). Although this last verse may be an editorial addition, it reflects the understanding that Isaiah's message includes the element of hope. Remember the name of Isaiah's older son: "A Remnant Shall Return."

This moderation, of course, says little about the personality of the prophet or what he thought should happen to the people who had forsaken their God. He is offering to the people the word of God, and it is their Lord, not Isaiah, who tempers justice with mercy and punishment with hope. Through the words of the prophet, we gain a glimpse more into the heart of God than the heart of Isaiah. Isaiah was simply the human voice through which God spoke.

Although the message is always moderated by hope, it is nonetheless clear and direct. Because Isaiah appears to have such ready access to political leaders, giving advice and exhortation to kings, it is assumed that he was a resident of Jerusalem and part of the upper class. He conformed to the classic definition of a prophet: someone who speaks truth to power. Always being scrupulous to announce that his word was coming from the Lord, he condemned every miscarriage of justice, especially as it related to the treatment of the poor. Only someone confident that his message had come from God could speak with this forthrightness to those in power:

Ah, you who make iniquitous decrees, who write oppressive statutes, to turn aside the needy from justice and to rob the poor of my people of their right, that widows may be your spoil, and that you may make the orphans your prey! What will you do on the day of punishment, in the calamity that will come from far away? To whom will you flee for help, and where will you leave your wealth, so as not to crouch among the prisoners or fall among the slain? For all this, [the Lord's] anger has not turned away; his hand is stretched out still. (Isa 10:1-4)

The noted Scottish preacher Phillips Brooks once defined preaching as "truth through personality" (14). Though the truth of the oracle always derives from Yahweh, the fiery personality and steely determination of the courageous prophet shine through.

Isaiah did not exclusively direct his message toward those in power. Von Rad points out that in Isaiah's time, legal decisions lay in the hands of the general body of citizens rather than those of legislators as we would think of them (120). Therefore, this message is not exclusively directed toward kings and judges. The people bear responsibility for their treatment of and care for each other. The sins against which Isaiah rails are collective sins brought about by the decisions of individual citizens. They cannot hide behind the excuse that their leaders were the ones in the wrong.

It is important to understand, however, that for Isaiah, the way justice was carried out in relation to the oppressed and defenseless was not so much a matter of relationship of human being to human being as of society's relationship to God. Because of the people's disobedience of God, Isaiah foresaw a complete breakdown in the societal order. The officials who held society together—judges, prophets, elder statesmen, military leaders, dignitaries, and counselors—would all disappear from the scene, leaving political neophytes and youngsters in charge (see Isaiah 3). Society fell apart not because of "man's inhumanity to man" but because of rebellion against the God who commanded them to take care of one another.

Isaiah's prediction of the future hope is depicted in civic terms. When Jerusalem is finally restored, it will be as a city-state, when God "will restore your judges as at the first, and your counselors as at the beginning. Afterwards you shall be called the city of righteousness, the faithful city" (Isa 1:26). It is understandable that, on the basis of proclamations such as this, the people of Jesus' day looked for a restoration of Israel in political terms. When the disciples asked Jesus, "Lord, is this the time when you will restore the kingdom to Israel?" (Acts 1:6), they may have been thinking specifically of the prophecies of Isaiah and the city-state concept he envisioned. This is particularly likely given the fact that, in his inaugural sermon recorded in Luke 4:16-21, Jesus takes as his text a passage from Isaiah, albeit a portion of the third section of the book (Isa 61:1, quoted by Luke directly from the Septuagint, the Greek translation of the Hebrew Scriptures):

> The Spirit of the Lord is upon me,
> because he has anointed me
> to bring good news to the poor.
> He has sent me to proclaim release to the captives
> and recovery of sight to the blind,
> to let the oppressed go free,
> to proclaim the year of the Lord's favor. (Luke 4:16-21)

The application of this text to himself indicates Jesus' understanding of the role he was to play as an interpretation and application of the prophetic words of Isaiah. Jesus interpreted "the restoration of Israel" as "a kingdom not of this world" (John 18:36), but his contemporaries would quite naturally hope for a more immediate change in the societal structure.

The Message of the Prophet

The central message of Isaiah's oracle is always absolute dependence on Yahweh. When political and military forces of foreign powers threatened the security of Judah, the temptation was to seek help from stronger nations. The strength of the covenant people was in their reliance on the One with whom they had formed the agreement in the first place. Any move to seek help elsewhere was a demonstration of their lack of faith in God.

When Hezekiah entered an alliance with Egypt because of the strength of Assyria, Isaiah warned, "The Egyptians are human, and not God; their horses are flesh, and not spirit. When the LORD stretches out his hand, the helper will stumble, and the one helped will fall, and they will all perish together" (Isa 31:3). Again there is the moderation of the message, however, with the reminder of the promise: "Like birds hovering overhead, so the LORD of hosts will protect Jerusalem; he will protect and deliver it, he will spare and rescue it. Turn back to him whom you have deeply betrayed, O people of Israel" (31:5).

For Isaiah, it was impossible for the people of Judah to have it both ways. The nation could not affirm dependence on God while seeking foreign alliances. When Ahaz was afraid because of the mounting pressure from Syria and Israel, Isaiah delivered this counsel from Yahweh: "Take heed, be quiet, do not fear, and do not let your heart be faint because of these two smoldering stumps of firebrands" (7:4b). Later, when Assyria threatened, this was the message: "For thus said the Lord GOD, the Holy One of Israel: In returning and rest you shall be saved; in quietness and in trust shall be your strength" (30:15). Then, as it has always been and always shall be, it was more difficult to remain quiet and accepting than to take action, no matter how futile that action might turn out to be. In the end, the people of Judah refused to put their faith in their God and so Jerusalem was destroyed.

Although Isaiah's message met with rejection in his own time, there is no indication that his faith in God's ultimate redemption of the people was shaken. Von Rad observes,

> Isaiah apparently acquiesced in the failure of his work. This he could do, because for him the word of Yahweh with which he was charged was beyond all criticism. If his own generation had rejected it, then it must be put in writing for a future one. The very fact that Isaiah did write it down makes clear that in his eyes the prophetic message was far from being a dead letter even if it had failed. (137)

Foreshadowing of the Destruction to Come

Contained within the first thirty-nine chapters of Isaiah are very few responses to Isaiah's message. Given the fact that, from the outset, God had told him that the people would not listen, this is hardly surprising. However, in the concluding scene of First Isaiah, there is a prototypical example of the reaction to his message. The thirty-ninth chapter opens with a new historical power on the scene, Babylon. At this point Babylon is subservient to Assyria but may be seeking a way out through an alliance with Judah. Hezekiah has been sick, almost to death, but, because of Hezekiah's imploring, God has granted him a reprieve and he is healed. The king of Babylon sends envoys to Hezekiah to congratulate him on his recovery.

In his enthusiasm to demonstrate his wealth and power, Hezekiah shows the envoys all the wealth of his kingdom: "Hezekiah welcomed them; he showed them his treasure-house, the silver, the gold, the spices, the precious oil, his whole armory, all that was found in his storehouses. There was nothing in his house or in all his realm that Hezekiah did not show them" (Isa 39:2). Given the dramatic, almost theatrical way in which this last scene is presented, you can almost see the envoys salivating over the booty that, as we know in retrospect, would one day belong to Babylon. As Brueggemann understates the case, "The review of resources may have been a routine act of policy-making. However, if we remember that in every international relationship the pattern of alliance and opposition changes often and quickly, we may judge that he committed a serious breach of security and discretion by disclosing too much to an ally not yet proven to be reliable" (1:311).

Apparently Isaiah was not present for this materialistic display, for when he hears about it he asks Hezekiah all about the encounter. Realizing that their opponents have seen all of the vast wealth of Judah, Isaiah informs Hezekiah that the Lord has a word for him: a time will come when all those things that have been stored up will belong to Babylon. Nothing will be left. Furthermore, some of his own sons will be taken away into Babylon and made eunuchs in the king's palace.

The response of Hezekiah, the final utterance of the material of First Isaiah, is almost beyond belief. Rather than taking this prophecy as a dark word of calamity and national crisis, Hezekiah responds, "'The word of the LORD that you have spoken is good.' For he thought, 'There will be peace and security in my days'" (Isa 39:8).

This profound and God-filled collection of oracles relating to the history of Yahweh with the people of Judah ends with the self-centered expression of relief of Hezekiah that, though terrible things may befall the descendants of the covenant, *even his own sons,* that calamity will be at some point in the future. There is no expression of regret that his actions may precipitate the crisis. There is no sadness over what will happen to his progeny. There is only personal relief that he will be spared. This is the final recorded response to the prophecies of Isaiah. It is an appropriate fulfillment of the oracle given to Isaiah at the time of his call: "Make the mind of this people dull, and stop their ears, and shut their eyes, so that they may not look with their eyes, and listen with their ears, and comprehend with their minds, and turn and be healed" (6:10).

1. The people of Judah felt threatened by their neighbors, causing anxiety and a sense of vulnerability. Summarize the threats, both internal and external, that could cause anxiety in our society.

_____

_____

_____

_____

_____

2. Isaiah was a central figure in the life of Judah, speaking truth to both the powerful and the common people. Could such a prophetic figure emerge today? What would limit that person's influence?

_____

_____

_____

_____

_____

3. Who might be some of the prophetic figures at work today?

_____

_____

_____

_____

_____

4. When Jesus preached, he spoke of "a kingdom not of this world." If as Christians our citizenship is in another world, what is our responsibility in working for the kinds of societal change Isaiah advocated in the name of God?

_____

_____

_____

_____

_____

5. If you were to have the access to political leaders Isaiah had, how would you speak "truth to power"? What would God want Christians to say to the president or members of Congress about the sources of strength on which we have come to rely?

_____

_____

_____

_____

_____

6. As Christians we believe the successor to the Israelites and their covenant with God is no single nation, but the church. Where does the church rely on earthly powers rather than on God?

_____

_____

_____

_____

_____

A Rebellious People

A particular phrase has made its way into the modern cultural vocabulary: *an inconvenient truth*. It refers to any fact that contradicts a theory or view one already firmly holds. Inconvenient truths often shatter our view of how things are supposed to be or how we have always thought they were. Being confronted with inconvenient truths is almost never pleasant, and it is human nature both to reject the truth and to react negatively toward anyone who forces us to confront it.

The people of Judah in the eighth through the sixth centuries BCE faced just such a crisis of thinking. Their worldview had been shaped in the time of Abraham, their ancestral father, and during the dynasty of David, their most revered king. They understood themselves to be engaged in a covenant relationship with Yahweh. Because of Abraham's faithfulness—to the point of being willing to sacrifice his son Isaac if that was what Yahweh asked—an agreement had been reached between the old patriarch and God. According to Genesis 17,

> When Abram was ninety-nine years old, the LORD appeared to Abram, and said to him, "I am God Almighty; walk before me, and be blameless. And I will make my covenant between me and you, and will make you exceedingly numerous." Then Abram fell on his face; and God said to him, "As for me, this is my covenant with you: You shall be the ancestor of a multitude of nations. No longer shall your name be Abram, but your name shall be Abraham; for I have made you the ancestor of a multitude of nations. I will make you exceedingly fruitful; and I will make nations of you, and kings shall come from you. I will establish my covenant between me and you, and your offspring after you

throughout their generations, for an everlasting covenant, to be God to you and to your offspring after you. And I will give you, and to your offspring after you, the land where you are now an alien, all the land of Canaan, for a perpetual holding; and I will be their God." (Gen 17:1-8)

This agreement between Yahweh and the descendants of Abraham, Isaac, and Jacob—the ancient patriarchs—held sway through the period of the great judges until, during the era of Samuel's judgeship, the people asked God for a king. God agreed to provide a monarch (although, according to 1 Samuel 8, Yahweh indicates this is a rejection of Yahweh as their king), and, after the disastrous experience with Saul, David ascended to the throne. When David took upon himself the plan of building a house for God, the Lord reminded him of the covenant between them:

[T]he LORD declares to you that the LORD will make you a house. When your days are fulfilled and you lie down with your ancestors, I will raise up your offspring after you, who shall come forth from your body, and I will establish his kingdom . . . . Your house and your kingdom shall be made sure for ever before me; your throne shall be established for ever. (2 Sam 7:11b-12).

After the death of David's son Solomon, the ancient nation of Israel split into the ten northern tribes of the kingdom of Israel and the two southern tribes of Judah and Benjamin. The southern kingdom, generally called the kingdom of Judah, with its capital in Jerusalem and containing Bethlehem, David's city, assumed the Davidic covenant continued through their monarchs. Because of these covenants, the collective worldview of the children of Israel, north and south, was their *exceptionalism*. As they understood these covenants, they were not like the other nations of the world. They had been chosen by God and promised security, property, and immortality. They would be safe from their enemies; they would call the land of promise their own, and their kingdom would never disappear.

A Contingent Covenant (Isaiah 1)

The *inconvenient truth* that most Israelites probably preferred to ignore was that this was a *contingent* covenant. The promise carried related expectations. These had been laid out as early as the time of Moses. After receiving the Ten Commandments a second time, Moses offers this exhortation to the people:

> So now, O Israel, what does the LORD require of you? Only to fear the LORD your God, to walk in all his ways, to love him, to serve the LORD your God with all your heart and with all your soul, and to keep the commandments of the LORD your God and his decrees that I am commanding you today, for your own well-being. Although heaven and the heaven of heavens belong to the LORD your God, the earth with all that is in it, yet the LORD set his heart in love on your ancestors alone and chose you, their descendants after them, out of all the peoples, as it is today. (Deut 10:12-15)

The covenant with Yahweh depended on the willingness of the people to adhere to the commandments of God and to be faithful to God alone. Note in the above passage from Genesis that God told Abraham to "walk before me and be blameless" (Gen 17:1). The agreement hinged on continued faithfulness to God. Though there is never a hint at a complete dissolution of the relationship from God's perspective, the quality of that relationship and the enjoyment of its benefits by the children of Israel always depended on their obeying the laws of Yahweh. And sometime in the eighth century BCE, a prophet named Isaiah began to point out both the failure of the people of Judah to fulfill their end of the bargain and the results of that failure.

The Sins that Broke the Covenant

Through the next two hundred years, others took up the mantle of Isaiah. They spoke in times of exile and crisis, but, following in the footsteps of the First Isaiah, they all spoke of the sins of Judah, the judgment that naturally followed, and Yahweh's redemptive plan. This first session will deal with the specific failings of the nation and God's judgment against them. Through this example of unwillingness to honor their covenant relationship, we may see how Christians, the followers of the new covenant, may also fail to live up to God's expectations.

While most of Isaiah 1–39 appears to have been written during or at least about events that occurred prior to the Babylonian exile, there has been some obvious editing of the material during a later age. The first chapter likely refers to events from several periods of Judah's history (Childs, 17), but they are all connected by the common theme of the nation's rebellion and punishment.

The prophecy opens with a stern and blunt reprimand of God's people. Although God has treated his people as children, they have rebelled against him. Whereas "The ox knows its owner, and the donkey its master's crib . . . Israel does not know, [God's] people do not understand" (Isa 1:3). This theme of willful ignorance will recur throughout the prophecy.

REJECTION OF THE LORD

In one powerful verse, 1:4, the nature of the people is laid bare, stripped of delusion or pretense of righteousness. In seven damning phrases, the oracle delivers God's clear picture of who God's chosen people have become:

- sinful nation
- people laden with iniquity
- offspring who do evil
- children who deal corruptly
- who have forsaken the LORD
- who have despised the Holy One of Israel
- who are utterly estranged

In that single verse, the writer characterizes the people of Judah as having completely abandoned their faith in God. As we will see, this rejection of the One with whom they were supposedly in covenant was graphically demonstrated by their worship of other gods, their treatment of the poor among them, their dependence on foreign alliances, and their obedience to wicked kings, but it is all summarized by a single word: rebellion.

INAUTHENTIC WORSHIP

This did not mean, however, that they no longer paid lip service to their reliance on God or that they had completely abandoned the practices of worship. At least during the time of the first prophet Isaiah, worship still centered on the temple in Jerusalem. If they needed any reminder that they were supposed to be in a special relationship with God, they had only to look for the smoke rising from the animal sacrifices made on their behalf in the temple. Priests were intervening for the Israelites with their God, asking for forgiveness of their sins. However, God saw the hypocrisy in their actions: "What to me is the multitude of your sacrifices? says the LORD; I have had enough of burnt-offerings of rams and the fat of fed beasts; I do not delight in the blood of bulls, or of lambs, or of goats" (1:11).

In as scathing a rejection of empty worship as is found anywhere in Scripture, Yahweh berates his children for trampling his courts, bringing futile offerings, burning abominable incense, strictly adhering to a calendar of worship without sincerity of practice, and engaging in solemn but hypocritical assemblies. Through the prophet, God was serving notice that the status quo was not acceptable. Their rebellion neither had escaped the notice of Yahweh nor would go unpunished.

In the chapters of Isaiah that follow, the prophet will go into graphic detail regarding the punishment they will face, but this much is clear: their rejection of Yahweh would result in Yahweh's rejection of them: "When you stretch out your hands," God said, "I will hide my eyes from you; even though you make many prayers, I will not listen; your hands are full of blood" (1:15).

When later generations languished and suffered in Babylonian captivity or struggled through the challenges of resettling in the land of Judah, they remembered these earlier oracles of warning and condemnation. The final composition of what became the biblical book of Isaiah was the result of wise spiritual and political leaders who sought to remind the battered and outcast people of Judah of where they had gone wrong and how they could be restored. By the time of Jesus, faithful Jews were looking for the fulfillment of promises of restoration and healing made in the prophecies of Isaiah.

The geographical center of God's relationship with Judah is Jerusalem. Walter Brueggemann remarks that the whole course of Jerusalem and the entire sequence of the book are laid out in 1:22-27 (Brueggemann, 1:2). Comparing the once-great city that was like silver to worthless metal and once like wine but now like water, Isaiah says that the leaders are "rebels and companions of thieves" (v. 22). Everyone loved bribes and ran after gifts while refusing to defend orphans and widows. The *inconvenient truth* was that their covenant relationship, now broken on the people's side, would not protect them from the wrath of Yahweh. God did not hold back: "Therefore says the Sovereign, the LORD of hosts, the Mighty One of Israel: Ah, I will pour out my wrath on my enemies, and avenge myself on my foes! I will turn my hand against you; I will smelt away your dross as with lye and remove all your alloy" (1:24-25).

Imagine how upsetting it must have been for people who were used to thinking of themselves as the children of God, the nation held in special relationship with the Almighty, to be called God's enemies and foes. They were being held to account, and, as the prophecy will make clear, the punishment would be severe.

The Offering of Hope (Isaiah 5)

Despite the stark warnings regarding sin and its punishment, from the outset of this prophecy there is always the word of hope. The people must change and offer penitence, but Yahweh will gladly accept them as God's own again. Isaiah lays out the practices of reform that could extricate the rebellious people from the mess they had made for themselves: "Wash yourselves; make yourselves clean; remove the evil of your doings from before my eyes; cease to do evil, learn to do good; seek justice, rescue the oppressed, defend the orphan, plead for the widow" (1:16-17).

And, in a poignant plea for the return of God's people to their Creator and Sustainer, the prophet offers this beautiful invitation:

> Come now, let us argue it out, says the LORD: though your sins are like scarlet, they shall be like snow; though they are red like crimson, they shall become like wool. If you are willing and obedient, you shall eat the good of the land; but if you refuse and rebel, you shall be devoured by the sword; for the mouth of the LORD has spoken. (1:18-20)

THE UNFRUITFUL VINEYARD

Many times through the first thirty-nine chapters of the prophecy we will find litanies of the sins of Israel, but the lyrics of a song found in the fifth chapter provide perhaps the most dramatic summation of all that Jerusalem has done wrong. Taking on the voice of Yahweh, the prophet sings "a love-song concerning my vineyard" (5:1). Notice that even though there is great sadness and regret, this is still a song of love. God's love for the people is like that of a vineyard keeper for his vineyard. With great care he clears the land and plants the choicest of vines, builds a watchtower, and hews out a wine vat. The vineyard keeper expectantly waits for a yield of good grapes, the natural product of his care. Instead, "it yielded wild grapes" (v. 2), a phrase descriptive of the rebellion of the people against their God.

Now Yahweh asks the people to judge for themselves how this could have happened. Since the vineyard keeper has done everything that could be expected of him, the yield of wild grapes is not his fault. "What more was there to do for my vineyard that I have not done for it?" God asks (v. 4). Therefore he will remove the hedge and break down the wall around it. He will allow it to be trampled, laid waste, and overrun with briars and thorns. In his sovereignty over nature, he will "command the clouds that they rain no rain upon it" (v. 6).

In the unlikely event that the metaphor escapes them, Yahweh spells it out: "For the vineyard of the LORD of hosts is the house of Israel, and the people of Judah are his pleasant planting; he expected justice, but saw bloodshed; righteousness, but heard a cry" (v. 7). In retrospect, the people of Judah could not avoid seeing the extended metaphor of the destroyed vineyard as an apt description of the historical events that eventually led to generations living in exile.

The remainder of the chapter, verses 8-30, is a list of specific sins the people have committed. The single word *u·ieiu* at the beginning of each of several condemning oracles is translated simply as "Ah" in the NRSV, but the Good News Bible gives the full sense of each paragraph by translating it "You are doomed" (5:8, 11, 18, 20, 21, 22).

The people stand accused of avaricious acquisition ("You . . . join house to house, . . . add field to field, until there is room for no one but you," v. 8); hedonism and drunkenness (v. 11); slavery to sin (v. 18); perverting of the truth (v. 20); and arrogance and pride (v. 21). While this may not be an exhaustive list of all the ways they had broken God's laws, it is a sufficient summary of the sins against which Isaiah will be called to prophesy.

The New Covenant and Another Inconvenient Truth

Christians hold that the covenant that Yahweh established with Israel was replaced with a new covenant given to those who willingly enter it through faith in Christ. At the Last Supper, the final meal that Jesus had with his disciples before his betrayal and crucifixion, he made clear this new connection between God and the faithful. The cup of wine that Jesus shared with his disciples represented the new covenant that was established "in his blood," that is, through his death (Matt 26:28; Mark 14:24; Luke 22:20).

The writer of the book of Hebrews saw Jesus as the "Great High Priest" who mediated this covenant between Yahweh and human beings. Harking back to Jeremiah, a contemporary prophet with the First Isaiah, the Hebrews author pointed out that it had been foretold that a new covenant would be established with the house of Israel and the house of Judah, "not like the covenant [Yahweh] made with their ancestors" (Heb 8:9). That prior covenant had been abrogated by the sins of the people, making a completely new one essential.

Now, with Jesus as "the mediator of a better covenant" (v. 6), "[Yahweh] will be their God, and they [the inheritors of the new covenant] shall be [Yahweh's] people" (v. 10). Through the life of the historical Jesus understood as the Messiah of God, Yahweh "has made the first one obsolete. And what is obsolete and growing old will soon disappear" (v. 13).

This understanding of the new covenant has led Christians to their own conclusion of *exceptionalism*, parallel to the claim of the ancient children of Judah. A common, indeed orthodox understanding of Christian belief is that the only way to attain a relationship with God is through faith in Jesus Christ. The proof text for this is John 14. There Jesus is seeking to prepare his disciples for the time when he will no longer be physically present among them. He tells them not only that he is going to prepare a place for them but also that he will come back to receive them. Furthermore, he tells them that they know where he is going. One of his disciples, Thomas, replies, "Lord, we do not know where you are going. How can we know the way?" (John 14:5).

Jesus' reply is the foundation of the Christian understanding of the exclusivity of Christ as the means of salvation: "I am the way, and the truth, and the life. No one comes to the Father except through me" (v. 6).

The implications of this claim are beyond the scope of this session. However, if one accepts this claim, as most Christians do, then it leads to the parallel *inconvenient truth* that this new covenant is *contingent* as well. While grace, the unmerited favor of God, is always available, and the relationship between God and human beings is not established through human goodness, willful disobedience causes estrangement and separation. The covenant into which individuals may voluntarily enter through faith in Christ can be strained, if not to the point of being broken, at least to the point of severe punishment.

In the time of persecution that followed the departure of Christ from the earth, a new prophet arose, John the Revelator, who wrote in exile on the Isle of Patmos. In his messages to the churches of Asia Minor, he included a revelation that he reported he had received from Christ to the church in Sardis, in which Christ reminded not only those Christians but all followers of Christ of their need to remain faithful:

> I know your works; you have a name for being alive, but you are dead. Wake up, and strengthen what remains and is at the point of death, for I have not found your works perfect in the sight of my God. Remember then what you received and heard; obey it, and repent. If you do not wake up, I will come like a thief, and you will not know at what hour I will come to you. Yet you have still a few people in Sardis who have not soiled their clothes; they will walk with me, dressed in white, for they are worthy. If you conquer, you will be clothed like them in white robes, and I will not blot your name out of the book of life; I will confess your name before my Father and before his angels. (Rev 3:1b-5)

Christians through the centuries have debated, on the basis of various Scripture passages, whether the covenant can be broken to the point where salvation is lost. Variously known as the eternal security of the believer, preservation of the saints, or "once saved, always saved," this doctrine can be either defended or argued against, depending on the Scriptures selected. Regardless of one's stance on this ultimate issue, the New Testament makes it clear that disobedience disappoints God and brings suffering to the believer, in this world if not in the next. If this understanding of the new covenant is similar to Isaiah's assessment of the old covenant, then Christians would do well to consider the critique Isaiah leveled against his people. Do the same inconvenient truths pertain today?

1. A covenant is an agreement or contract between two persons or groups, with each promising to do something in relationship with the other. Summarize the covenant relationship between God and the people of Judah as it was understood at the time of the beginning of the prophecy of Isaiah.

_____

_____

_____

_____

_____

2. Since the time of the historical Jesus, the church—the body of Christ on earth—has been in a similar covenant with God. State the terms of that covenant as you understand them.

_____

_____

_____

_____

_____

3. Each individual Christian enters into a covenantal agreement with God at the time of accepting Christ as Savior. How would you describe that covenant in your own life?

_____

_____

_____

_____

_____

4. The opening chapters of Isaiah list in great detail the sins of Israel that anger God and that will result in their punishment. What similarities do you see between the sins listed in chapters 1 and 5 and the violations of God's will in our culture?

_____

_____

_____

_____

_____

5. For personal reflection: As you read chapters 1 and 5, what judgment does this bring to your own conduct?

_____

_____

_____

_____

_____

6. One of the specific sins of Judah that concerned Isaiah was inauthentic worship. He said that the people were going through the motions of offering worship to God but were insincere. What evidence do you see that some practices of worship today may be inauthentic?

_____

_____

_____

_____

_____

7. Judah faced the inconvenient truth that, though they were God's chosen, their conduct could separate them from God. Review your own conduct and list the actions in which you might engage that would displease God and thus lead to separation from God.

_____

_____

_____

_____

_____

A Holy God

Session

Isaiah 6

The first five chapters of the book of Isaiah comprise a litany of collective sinfulness, rebellion, and covenant violation. However, as is true in almost all assessments of cultural condition, exceptions emerge. Individuals refuse to conform to the conduct of the larger community. The sixth chapter of the book of Isaiah is an account of one man's realization of his own sinfulness and his distancing himself from the ways of his people. In the midst of shame and confrontation with harsh reality, one man hears and accepts the call of Yahweh. Isaiah becomes a prophet who will accept the commission to carry a word from the Lord to the people of Judah.

Chapter 6, and perhaps all the way through chapter 9, is a memoir, a personal account of Isaiah's experiences during the crisis arising from the threat to Judah from Syria and Israel and a retrospective account of his call. More important, however, it is a description of a personal encounter with a holy God.

A Vision of Heaven and Earth

Isaiah dates the time of his call "In the year that King Uzziah died" (Isa 6:1). There is some disagreement among historians as to the year when that occurred, possibly 742 or 736. Brevard Childs notes that the significance of that event was more than the death of the monarch. It marked a turning point in God's history with God's people (54–55). Walter Brueggemann, however, suggests that mentioning the death may serve only "to contrast the transitoriness of human kings with the abiding quality of the divine king" (1:58).

While for some time the people of Judah may have thought of God as being some distance removed from them, God was about to intervene in a personal, dramatic, and catastrophic way. God's tolerance of the sinfulness of the people was about to end, and they would face the consequences of their rebellion and the breaking of their covenant. And the proclaiming of that message begins with a heavenly vision to an individual who receives a call.

Isaiah recounts how in the year of the king's death he "saw the LORD sitting on a throne, high and lofty" (Isa 6:1). While this image of an elevated throne clearly conveys a vision of God's heavenly dwelling, "the hem of his robe filled the temple." This is a graphic depiction of the God who rules over both heaven and earth. God's personhood and dominion stretch from the highest reaches of heaven to the lowest points of earth. When Isaiah described what he had seen, those who conceived of Yahweh as distant and removed would see that their God was among them. On the other hand, for those who had gotten too familiar in their understanding of their relationship with the Deity, this image clearly attests to God's holiness and majesty.

The description Isaiah offers strongly suggests he was participating in an earthly service of communal worship during which this picture of the divine presence was presented to him. References to the door posts, smoke (incense or smoke from the sacrificial offerings), and altar all ground the experience in the physical location where people were supposed to worship God, but where God "had enough of burnt offerings of rams and the fat of fed beasts" (1:11b). Isaiah was either in the temple or at least engaged in reverie about that holy building when he received this vision.

In its earthly dimension, Isaiah may have heard the temple choir singing an antiphonal anthem, calling out to one another, "Holy, holy, holy is the LORD of hosts; the whole earth is filled with his glory" (v. 3). Certainly many choirs since have sung these words in anthems that may approach heavenly beauty and that would indeed "shake the pivots on the thresholds" (v. 4a). There is an emotional response to music, particularly as it conveys the holiness and majesty of God. Worshipers of every age have been moved to a sense of God's presence by sacred music, and this situation may well have enhanced the vision of Isaiah.

Further grounding the vision in immediate reality, the smoke from the offerings would have filled the house, a symbol of the presence of God. The Christian Scriptures used the same symbolism in depicting heavenly worship in the book of Revelation: "And the temple was filled with smoke from the glory of God and from his power" (Rev 15:8a). Isaiah is aware that he is not merely participating in a communal exercise but has been ushered into the presence of Yahweh, a presence that is pervasive throughout the temple.

The cumulative effect of these sensations—of elevated presence and song and smoke—is to create an awareness of the holiness of God, a radical otherness from the human beings God has made. Brueggemann calls this "the holiness, the splendor, the glory, the unutterable majesty of the ruler of heaven whose awesome governance extends over all the earth" (1:58–59). Childs notes that the glory to which the seraphs refer is God's "disclosed holiness; his holiness is his inner glory. . . . Holiness in the Old Testament is not an ethical quality, but the essence of God's nature as separate and utterly removed from the profane" (55). It is this holiness that causes awe in God's servants and, in this particular instance, strikes fear in Isaiah's heart.

Isaiah's Call as Commentary on Worship

Today the conversation about worship in Christian churches tends to focus on matters of style—contemporary or traditional, formal or informal, organ and choir or praise band. The differences seem to relate to questions of personal preference. What style of music do we *like*? What sort of setting makes us *comfortable*? What level of personal participation do we *want*? The danger in viewing worship purely from the human side is that we might have an experience of our own selves but not an encounter with God. The more appropriate question to ask of worship is, were the senses engaged and the elements of worship presented in such a way that I became *aware of the presence and the holiness of God*? Our own experiences of worship, without regard to context or style, simply cannot be considered on the same plane with Isaiah's unless there is a clear, indisputable sense of the presence of God.

In Isaiah's account of his encounter in the temple and in every experience of authentic worship, the result is an inevitable awareness of one's own sinfulness. Isaiah cries out, "Woe is me! I am lost, for I am a man of unclean lips, and I live among a people of unclean lips; yet my eyes have seen the King, the LORD of hosts!" (Isa 6:5). In the presence of a holy God, he is aware of the contrast of his own sinfulness and his complicity in the sinfulness of his people. Furthermore, he has seen the King, not some earthly ruler like Uzziah, but the ruler of heaven and earth who sits on the throne above and still has a decided interest in the conduct of those below.

A Holy God

This element of confession, the acknowledgment of our own unworthiness to be in the presence of a holy God, may be the feature of worship most noticeably absent from the contemporary Christian experience. Either admission of our guilt is incorporated as rote "Unison Confession of Sin," devoid of all specificity of personal transgression, or it is absent altogether as we lustily affirm the awesomeness of God without seeing our own human frailty and failing. Without this confession, there is no motivation for seeking cleansing. We may leave the worship experience with a vague feeling of well-being but no radical change offered through the forgiveness and empowerment of God.

Confession that Leads to Cleansing

Once Isaiah has cried out in despondent confession, the agent of God, the seraph, takes over. It is in Isaiah's account of this cleansing that the prophet is the most specific and dramatic. He envisions one of the heavenly creatures touching his mouth with a coal taken from the altar fire. So often in the Old Testament, especially in the Psalms, fire is seen as representing the wrath of God, but here it cleanses Isaiah's mouth, the vehicle through which he will convey the word of God to God's people. The words of the seraph form the basis for the classic declaration of pardon still used in worship: "Now that this has touched your lips, your guilt has departed and your sin is blotted out" (v. 7). This experience of an individual will provide another reminder to those who will hear it or read it later that, despite their rebellion, there is the option of confession that results in cleansing. Isaiah is providing personal testimony that "though your sins are like scarlet, they shall be like snow; though they are red like crimson, they shall become like wool" (Isa 1:18b).

The spiritual descendants of Isaiah, the followers of Jesus Christ in the earliest churches, heard similar words of assurance of God's pardon once they had confessed their sins. The Apostle Paul wrote,

> But now, apart from law, the righteousness of God has been disclosed, and is attested by the law and the prophets, the righteousness of God through faith in Jesus Christ for all who believe. For there is no distinction, since all have sinned and fall short of the glory of God; and they are now justified by his grace as a gift, through the redemption that is in Christ Jesus. (Rom 3:21-24)

The Voice of God

It is only when Isaiah's mouth has been cleansed that he hears the voice of God. More accurately, he overhears God consulting with his heavenly assistants. Although most often this encounter is described as the calling of Isaiah, it could be more precise to say that in this experience Isaiah recognizes the holiness of God, confesses his sin in God's presence, receives the cleansing that God provides, and then volunteers for a job God needs to have done. There is no sense in the narrative that Isaiah has been singled out or chosen. He simply responds to the question, "Whom shall I send, and who will go for us?" (v. 8). It is as if he has walked in on a conversation already underway and is so moved by what is occurring that he almost impetuously responds with, "Here am I; send me!" Apparently at this point he has no idea to whom he is to be sent or the content of the message. He only knows that now he is ready to go.

A Model for Worship

Many commentators have seen Isaiah's experience as an outline for proper worship as it should be practiced today. There are the elements of praise (depicted as angelic beings calling out to one another in vv. 1-4), confession (v. 5), extending of forgiveness (vv. 6-7), and sending out to serve (v. 8). Although modern liturgists may not feel bound by these elements in the construction of corporate worship events, together they lead to attaining the goal of all worship: an experience of the holy. The various elements, however, must be seen as part of a cohesive whole. Focusing on any one of these elements to the exclusion of the others results in an incomplete experience of the relationship between Creator and creatures.

A worship experience consisting almost exclusively of *praise* fails to take into account the responsibility of the worshiper to examine himself or herself in the light of the wholly other God who is being worshiped. True experience of the holiness of God naturally results in despair about one's own condition of sinfulness.

To focus on *confession of sin* without following immediately with some declaration of pardon based on the expression of sorrow over one's actions leaves the worshiper guilt-ridden and still sorrowful. As Frederick Buechner observed, what we proclaim "is sad news before it is glad news" (23). But it cannot remain sad news only. There must be the good and glad news that there is no sin beyond the possibility of God's forgiveness. Modern preachers who concentrate on the enumeration of sins (often those of "the world" outside the church) do a disservice to their hearers if there is not an immediate and clear reminder that there is always hope for forgiveness to all who seek a restored relationship.

Conversely, to extend on behalf of God the *offering of forgiveness* without insisting on the element of confession can lead to what Dietrich Bonhoeffer so aptly called "cheap grace," where we gladly accept the assurance of God's pardon without fully realizing the magnitude of our personal sins that makes such forgiveness necessary.

Finally, *sending out to serve* must be more than a lecture on the necessity of following Christ's example or a general challenge to go out into the world to minister in some vague way. Rather, service is the natural response of a forgiven person to the grace of God. One goes to others on behalf of God because he or she has received a gift that is meant to be shared.

The drama of worship, so beautifully displayed in the call of Isaiah, always contains several movements that follow in natural progression and are mutually dependent on one another—not simply for a complete experience but so that the cry might finally come forth: "Send me!"

The Prophetic Commission

We have already been made privy to the content of the message with which Isaiah will be entrusted. In the fifth chapter of Isaiah, we have seen the image of the vineyard that will be destroyed. We know God will respond to the unfaithfulness of the people with anger. The enemy that will be the tool of God's wrath is already poised for attack. This is the message with which Isaiah begins his oracle, but in chapter 6 he is writing in retrospect. When he received the holy vision, he did not yet know a turning point had been reached in Yahweh's relationship with Yahweh's people. We can only imagine his visceral response to the directions he was then given.

The human expectation of what the content of the message Isaiah was to deliver, especially given the promise of the possibility of repentance and forgiveness in the first chapter, would be both warning and the possibility of hope. However, no such hope is forthcoming in the message presented to Isaiah. Instead, it appears Isaiah is to be the instrument through which Israel's lack of response to the love of God is hardened. He is to tell them that they should keep listening but that they will not understand. The preaching of the prophet will "make the minds of this people dull" (Isa 6:10a). All of their senses will be deadened. And the shocking point is that, if this did not happen, they would understand the nature of their sin and God's willingness to forgive and would "turn and be healed" (v. 10). Would not Isaiah (in fact, would not *we*) think that repentance was precisely what God desired?

The message needs to be received, however, within the larger context of the preaching of the First Isaiah. While Isaiah 1–39 are clear in their warning of what is to come, and the remainder of the book contains words of comfort to those who have suffered for their rebellion, the overall message of all sixty-six chapters is hope. This hope may not be realized in the lifetimes of any of the original hearers of the oracle, or even of the returning exiles, but God will redeem God's people.

Christopher Seitz interprets this passage as a pastoral message directed specifically to Isaiah and delivered in the midst of the divine council:

> Isaiah is not to interpret the refusal to hear, which comes as a result of his preaching, as a sign of his failure or as an indication of divine malfeasance. The prophet learns from God that he will make hearts fat with the effect that the people will not turn and be healed. God lets him know this at a critical moment in his career, as he is about to leave the divine council. (Seitz, 56)

Although this seems to be a judgment against the stubbornness of the people of Judah, Brevard Childs warns against trying to shift the initiative for this hardening to them. In the Old Testament, "the hard juxtaposition of divine initiative and Israel's guilt remains unmoved" (Childs, 56). This is not simply a conditional statement (i.e., if God's people harden their hearts, they will experience God's wrath). In the Old Testament, hardening of the heart is always represented as an act of God and not as the result of human action (von Rad, 123). Childs does point out, however, that this is a message specifically for that moment in history to the particular people of sinful Israel. We should not make any broader implication to God hardening hearts in any general way that would make them resistant to the overall message of hope and redemption evident throughout the Bible.

When Isaiah hears this negative message, he does not try to argue with God or ask why it must be so. Instead he adopts the language of the Psalms: "How long, O LORD?" (v. 11). The answer that he receives is that this estrangement will be of a lengthy but not interminable time. The cities of Judah will be laid waste and their inhabitants carried away into captivity. The land will be utterly desolate. If this vision is indeed included as part of a larger memoir, Isaiah must have been looking back on a career spent offering hope in the midst of hopelessness, counseling trust in the face of seeming abandonment, and looking for redemption in a time when salvation seemed very far away.

There is, however, in the final line of this prophetic oracle, a foreshadowing of the plan of God to save God's people. Although Judah will be burned and burned again like a tree whose stump remains standing when it is felled, "The holy seed is its stump" (v. 13b). Although this hopeful sentence may not have been part of the original message, it at least marks the understanding of later interpreters that, even in the midst of God's response to the rebellion of the people, there was the glimmer of hope. This last word does not soften the terrible judgment of the oracle but allows it to be seen in the greater realm of the providence of God, a realm that both Jews and later Christians saw as offering of hope at any point where one turned from sin and back to God.

A New Covenant Parallel

A few centuries later, another figure appeared in the area around Jerusalem whose life resonated with the call of Isaiah to speak to people whose ears were closed and hearts were hardened to the message of Yahweh's love. All four Gospels record accounts of Jesus of Nazareth preaching to crowds who gathered in response to the performing of miracles but who never accepted the "hard sayings" of sacrifice and total commitment that were required of his disciples.

In Matthew 13 and the parallels in Mark 4 and Luke 8, Jesus had attracted such a great crowd around a lake that he had to get in a boat and push off from shore as the people gathered on the beach. As he began to speak, rather than remark on the great size of the crowd, he told a parable of a sower whose efforts resulted in only a small portion of the seed he threw out ever taking root. When the disciples asked him why he spoke in such parabolic fashion, he quoted Isaiah 6:9-10 almost word for word, linking the lack of demonstrable response to his preaching to the same response to Isaiah's message. Indeed, Jesus sees this response as a *fulfillment* of the message that Isaiah received in the context of his call. (See Matt 13:1-17; Mark 4:1-20; Luke 8:1-10.)

In the twelfth chapter of the Gospel of John, the evangelist notes that "Although [Jesus] had performed many signs in their presence, they did not believe in him" (John 12:37). Rather than having Jesus quote the passage from Isaiah, John simply says "This was to fulfill the word spoken by the prophet Isaiah" and then connects a passage from the Second Isaiah, "Who has believed what we have heard? And to whom has the arm of the LORD been revealed?" (53:1), with 6:9-10, "'Keep listening, but do not comprehend; keep looking, but do not understand.' Make the mind of this people dull, and stop their ears, and shut their eyes, so that they may not look with their eyes, and listen with their ears, and comprehend with their minds, and turn and be healed." Then pointedly John remarks, "Isaiah said this because he saw his glory and spoke about him" (John 12:41).

Luke picks up this theme in his companion work to the Gospel, the book of Acts. At the end of his history of the early formations of the Christian church, he records a sermon preached by the Apostle Paul to Jewish leaders in Rome. When many of them refused to respond positively to his proclamation of the gospel, he remarked, "The Holy Spirit was right in saying to your ancestors through the prophet Isaiah," and then quotes Isaiah 6:9-10. He concludes, "Let it be known to you then that this salvation of God has been sent to the Gentiles; they will listen" (Acts 28:23-30).

Have Our Hearts Become Hardened?

The oracle that the First Isaiah was given for the people of Judah could be distilled as "enough is enough." Yahweh had shown patience in the face of resistance to unfailing love and outright rebellion against the demand for exclusive obedience. The "people of the covenant" had been warned again and again that continuing rebellion would result in rejection and punishment. God never took delight in their discipline; it was simply the direct consequence of their actions.

There are parallels in the experience of many Christians. As recipients of the new covenant, we have experienced grace and favor. However, this has not always prevented us from continuing in rebellion and overt sin. Modern prophets and preachers have warned that there are consequences to such actions. The question that we must consider is whether or not, through a casual approach to worship, an unwillingness to acknowledge our sins, and the deafness that comes after repeated warnings, our hearts have also been hardened to the call for repentance. Might we find ourselves on the brink of being given up to the tragedy of exile? There is much to learn from the experience of the children of Israel.

1. Isaiah lived in a culture of sinfulness and rebellion against God, yet he was able to experience God's presence and respond to the excesses around him. What do you see as the most prevalent sins of our culture, and how can you stand apart from them?

_____

_____

_____

_____

_____

2. Isaiah's call appears to have taken place in the context of a service of worship. As you review the elements of that experience (praise, confession, forgiveness, commitment), how do you see those elements incorporated into the worship services in which you participate today?

_____

_____

_____

_____

_____

3. If you were to be involved in the planning of worship, how would you seek to incorporate these features in order to create an awareness of the holy?

_____

_____

_____

_____

_____

4. The prophet Isaiah voluntarily responded to the call of God for someone to go to the people of Judah. Who are the groups of people—family, coworkers, neighbors, friends—to whom God might be sending you?

_____

_____

_____

_____

_____

5. As you think about these various people in your life, what do you believe God might want you to say to each of them?

_____

_____

_____

_____

_____

6. As you think about your own religious experience, there may have been a time, perhaps in the midst of a moving worship service, when you responded, either publicly or internally, with a commitment to service. Have you kept that commitment? How has your understanding of that commitment changed over the years?

_____

_____

_____

_____

_____

7. For personal reflection: Is it possible that you have heard the words of warning about the consequences of rebellion so often that they no longer have an impact on your life?

_____

_____

_____

_____

_____

A Holy God

A Sign of Hope

The understanding of the term "messiah" is of critical importance for Christian faith. Most believers have some concept of what it means for the historical Jesus to be the Messiah ("Christ" is the Greek equivalent), the fulfillment of the prophecies of the Hebrew Scriptures relating to a deliverer sent by Yahweh to rescue God's people from bondage. Many do not, however, understand the context in which that concept first arose.

At Caesarea Philippi, when Jesus asked his disciples who they believed him to be, Peter's response was, "You are the Christ (Messiah), the Son of the Living God" (Matt 16:16). He was connecting Jesus with the expectation of Israel that there would be one to come to save God's people. Peter apparently had no idea, however, how radically different Jesus' understanding of the application of that term was from his own. In Matthew's account, although Jesus affirmed that Peter had answered well, as soon as Jesus began to inform the disciples that he would suffer, "Peter took him aside and began to rebuke him" (16:21a). It was simply beyond Peter's ability to conceive that the deliverer would redeem the people through suffering rather than worldly triumph.

Christians now have the benefit of hindsight. Through the New Testament witnesses, we are able to understand that it was precisely through the suffering and sacrificial death on the cross that Jesus became the Christ, the One who would deliver people not from earthly bondage but from sin and death. However, just as Peter did not understand the new interpretation, Christians do not always understand the background of the original meaning from which it arose. The idea of a Suffering Servant that Jesus applied to himself arises out of the oracles of Isaiah. The First Isaiah spoke of one who would be the symbol of hope. Those who wrote what became the second portion of the book of Isaiah received a word from Yahweh about how the servant whom Yahweh called would suffer. Jesus connected the two concepts within his own life. In this section, we will see this messianic idea as a sign of hope for all times and all people, but arising from the life of the people of Israel.

If You Do Not Stand Firm in Faith . . .

The seventh chapter of Isaiah records an encounter between the prophet and King Ahaz that was to have significance far beyond the immediate situation. The seed for one of the central tenets of both Jewish and Christian faith, the coming of the Messiah of Yahweh, was first sown in a time of political crisis and weakening resolve among the people of Judah, eight centuries before the birth of Jesus. The city of Jerusalem was under threat of attack from the northern neighbors of Syria and Israel, and fear was in the air. As Isaiah expresses it, "the heart of Ahaz and the heart of his people shook as the trees of the forest shake before the wind" (Isa 7:2b). As the scene opens, King Ahaz is inspecting the vulnerable waterworks, probably because he was expecting the city soon to be under siege. Displaying the lack of faith in God's protection that we have already discussed, the king is considering making an appeal to Assyria, the far more powerful empire to the north of Israel and Syria. The fact that Ahaz is contemplating the possibility of appealing to the more serious threat of Assyria as a way of avoiding conflict with the two less powerful enemies, Syria and Israel, is a clear indication of the young king's level of panic.

Stating what must have already been obvious to the young king, Isaiah pointed out that it was *Jerusalem* that was under threat of siege. This is of particular importance because Jerusalem was not some isolated, insignificant part of the land of Judah. It was the seat of the royal family, the line of David. In the second verse, Isaiah writes that it was not simply Ahaz, the current king, but also "the house of David" that had learned of this threat. More than a military conflict, this crisis threatened the line of kings established by Yahweh. Isaiah went out to meet Ahaz, but the king may not have found comfort in the fact that the prophet was accompanied by his son, Shear-jashub, "a remnant shall return." It is doubtful that Ahaz wanted to be reminded that the prophet's oracle included the prospect of hope for later generations but destruction of city and dynasty in the immediate future.

Nevertheless, it was a word of comfort that Isaiah sought to give to the young king. He instructed him in the proper stance of one who depends on Yahweh for protection: "Take heed, be quiet, do not fear, and do not let your heart be faint . . ." (7:4). For God to be involved in the affairs of Judah would require a stillness that renounces aid from earthly sources. Isaiah told him that the two national powers that he saw as such a threat were no more than the burning embers of trees already cut down. Although the son who accompanied Isaiah was "A Remnant Shall Return," the one more closely tied to the events of the moment was the second son whose birth would be announced in the next chapter: "The Spoil Speeds, the Prey Hastens." Very soon, Assyria would be gathering the spoils from the prey of Syria and Israel. However, Judah would not gain by aligning with the victor in this particular battle. They would do well to remain on the sidelines of this conflict, trusting that God would keep them from harm. Challenging the monarch with the central theme of all his prophecy, Isaiah reminded him, "If you do not stand firm in faith, you shall not stand at all" (v. 9b). The future of the line of Davidic kings and of the city of Jerusalem would depend on faith.

Again the *Contingent* Covenant

Notice that Isaiah was again underscoring the *contingency of the covenant.* God's protection rests on the continuing faithfulness of God's people. Though Syria and Damascus would not prevail, the protection of Jerusalem depended on reliance on Yahweh. This condition may have been a rude awakening for the king. Yahweh's protection since the time of David had been something the monarchs and the people took for granted. They felt that as the favored children of God they could do no wrong. Now Isaiah reminds them they must be obedient if they expect protection.

This is another example of the *inconvenient truth* with which we began. Yahweh protects the people when they remain faithful. When the covenant is broken, divine protection is withdrawn. This incident marks the turning point in the understanding of the relationship between God and God's people. Childs underscores the critical nature of this exchange when he notes, "In a word, unless Judah, the people of God, understands itself as a theological reality—a creation of God and not merely a political entity—the state will have no future existence" (64). While Ahaz was focused on an immediate threat to his kingship, the prophet stood as a reminder that something greater was at stake than one man's legacy.

The Sign of Immanuel

As further assurance of Yahweh's abiding interest in Judah's affairs, Isaiah offered Ahaz the opportunity to ask for a sign. Ahaz refused the offer, saying that he would not put God to the test. He would seem to be on solid theological ground here. In Deuteronomy 6:16, the Torah asserts, "Do not put the LORD your God to the test, as you tested him at Massah." This refers to the incident from the exodus period when the Israelites complained about the lack of water. Moses warned them about trying to force God into doing their bidding. The spot was thus named Massah, the Hebrew word for "testing." This was the passage Jesus quoted when, during the wilderness temptation scene (Matt 4:7 and Luke 4:12), Satan tried to induce Jesus to jump from the parapet of the temple to demonstrate his power.

So it seems that Ahaz was being pious when he refused to test God by asking for a sign. However, judging from Isaiah's reaction ("Is it too little for you to weary mortals, that you weary my God also?"), the refusal was really an indication of Ahaz's determination to go ahead with a foreign alliance. He was being hypocritical by pretending to honor God, when in fact he was displaying a lack of faith in Yahweh's ability to do anything about their vulnerable situation. Ahaz needed no sign of God's power because he had no intention of depending on it. Isaiah was angry about the continued refusal to place his faith in the only source of genuine rescue.

Although Ahaz would not ask for a sign, the Lord gave him one of God's own choosing:

> Look, the young woman is with child and shall bear a son, and shall name him Immanuel. He shall eat curds and honey by the time he knows how to refuse the evil and choose the good. For before the child knows how to refuse the evil and choose the good, the land before whose two kings you are in dread will be deserted. The LORD will bring on you and on your people and on your ancestral house such days as have not come since the day that Ephraim departed from Judah—the king of Assyria. (Isa 7:14b-17)

Regardless of the use of this promise in later Christian thought, as in the use of the name "Immanuel" in Matthew 1:23, the original intention of the oracle is clearly to be applied to the immediate and future context of the house of David. Because of the refusal of Ahaz to place his faith in Yahweh, Judah will see such destruction as has not been seen since the original division of Israel. They will be defeated by the Assyrians, all because of Ahaz's fear of the lesser powers of Syria and Israel and their lack of faith in Yahweh. In the face of crisis, Ahaz chooses the wrong path.

Although considerable scholarship has been devoted to the "young woman" (*almâ*) who will bear the child, little can be determined from the context or events that followed. The phrase refers to any young woman of marriageable age. The emphasis of this oracle is on the child, not the mother. The later interest of the Christian church in interpreting the mother as a virgin is simply not the interest of the prophecy as originally transmitted. The point is that this tragedy will befall Judah before a child reaches an age where he can know moral responsibility.

Once again, as with the names of Isaiah's sons, the name "Immanuel" is full of meaning. Although Jerusalem will be laid to waste, there will be a child whose name, "God with us," bears testimony to the faithfulness of God in spite of the faithlessness of the king and of the people. This child's life will mark the time of the immediate threat. By the time he has reached the ability to know right from wrong, perhaps by the age of two, the crisis will have passed. Ahaz is deeply concerned about trouble that will soon be over, while displaying disregard for the far greater threat of abandoning hope in Yahweh. This is the formula for the disaster that would soon befall Judah.

We now read this passage through the lens of history, and particularly through our knowledge of the application of this text to the role of the historical Jesus. Matthew seized upon this event out of the history of his people as a foreshadowing of the part that Jesus was to play in the events, not only of the historical period marked by Roman domination but also throughout history. God is again providing hope in the midst of desperate circumstances, not just for the restored nation of Israel living under Roman rule but for all people of all ages. "God with us" is an affirmation of Yahweh's presence in every time and place.

The part that Ahaz plays in this drama is reenacted over and over again in the lives of individuals. How often have we become so obsessed with an immediate crisis that we sought whatever help was at hand rather than trusting in the faithfulness of God? The issue that caused us such grief may soon be over, but our relationship with God is damaged by our unwillingness to trust our Creator. For those of us who are Christians, the promise of "God with Us" in Jesus should be a constant reminder that God remains faithful, but our well-being depends on trust.

A Child Has Been Born for Us

Apart from Psalm 23, the portion of Hebrew poetry with which Christians are most familiar may be the ninth chapter of Isaiah:

> The people who walked in darkness
>   have seen a great light;
> those who lived in a land of deep darkness—
>   on them light has shined.
> You have multiplied the nation,
>   you have increased its joy;
> they rejoice before you
>   as with joy at the harvest,
>   as people exult when dividing plunder.
> For the yoke of their burden,
>   and the bar across their shoulders,
>   the rod of their oppressor,
>   you have broken as on the day of Midian.
> For all the boots of the tramping warriors
>   and all the garments rolled in blood
>   shall be burned as fuel for the fire.
> For a child has been born for us,
>   a son given to us;
> authority rests upon his shoulders;
>   and he is named
> Wonderful Counselor, Mighty God,
>   Everlasting Father, Prince of Peace.
> His authority shall grow continually,
>   and there shall be endless peace
> for the throne of David and his kingdom.
>   He will establish and uphold it
> with justice and with righteousness
>   from this time onward and forevermore.
> The zeal of the LORD of hosts will do this. (Isaiah 9:2-7)

Though Christians inevitably connect this beautiful lyric poem with the birth of Jesus, it is important that we understand its original context. Isaiah 9:2-7 has been placed in the collected oracles following the sign of the Assyrian invasion contained in the naming of Isaiah's second son in chapter 8. This is preceded in chapter 7 by the confrontation between Ahaz and Isaiah in which the king chose to place his faith in Assyrian protection rather than in Yahweh. Given its location, it is natural to understand that this poem, which speaks of a future king far better than Ahaz, is referring to Hezekiah, the son of Ahaz, who restored a time of prosperity after the disaster of the Assyrian alliance. While it is included in the chronology as a prediction of future action, the people of Judah who lived through the contrasting reigns of Ahaz and Hezekiah would have interpreted it as prophecy now fulfilled. No matter how we might interpret this passage as a reference to Jesus, the natural reading at the time would be as a reference to Hezekiah. The original readers of the oracles compiled in what we know as the book of Isaiah, living centuries before the birth of Jesus, would look to the reign of Hezekiah as a time of "great light" after the disastrous years under Ahaz.

Second Chronicles 29 describes the reforms of Hezekiah. During the reign of Ahaz, the temple had been closed and the worship of foreign gods had been allowed. One of Hezekiah's first acts upon assuming the throne was to repair and reopen the temple. He abolished idolatry and destroyed some of the pagan worship centers. He also attempted to establish better relations with the northern kingdom of Israel by inviting worshipers to return to Jerusalem for Passover, but his invitation was rejected out of hand. Nevertheless, he oversaw the celebration of this reminder of Israelite history with great solemnity. He brought the people back to their roots, planted in the soil of the first exile in Egypt and their return to the land of promise. For devout Jews who saw allegiance to Yahweh as the source of Judah's well-being, these reforms must have truly seemed like a time of light after darkness.

It is not necessary, however, to see the poem solely in that context. The children of Judah in exile may have read this lyrical work in terms of the time prior to and during the exile and the postexilic era. The introductory verse 1 delineates between "the former time" when Yahweh brought the land low because of the unfaithfulness of the people and "the latter time" when the glory of "the land beyond the Jordan" will be restored. Whatever reforms and relative prosperity the people might have experienced under Hezekiah, for Jews living in Babylon those days were long past. Their concern was with how they might be delivered from their present troubles. They continued to look for a deliverer. The remnant who returned to Jerusalem following the exile must have read this passage also and continued to look for a new leader who would restore their former glory.

In a later age, the followers of Jesus of Nazareth saw him as the fulfillment of this prophecy. The Gospel writer Matthew makes this connection when he discloses that Jesus made his home in Capernaum, a city in the region of Zebulon and Naphtali, the place that Isaiah said the one to come would make glorious. Matthew then points to Jesus as the one who marks a pivotal point in history: "The people who sat in darkness have seen a great light, and for those who sat in the region and shadow of death light has dawned" (Matt 4:16), an almost direct quote of Isaiah 9:2. For Matthew, the Gospel writer most concerned with the fulfillment of Old Testament prophecy, Jesus is the righteous king whom Isaiah said would come.

Similarly, the adoption of this poem by later Christians as applying to Jesus as the Christ is beyond the original historical context. Most assuredly, when the words "Unto us a child is born, unto us a son is given" are sung as part of Handel's *Messiah*, neither the musicians nor the members of the audience are thinking of either Hezekiah or a leader of postexilic Judah. There is a reason this work is included in the Christmas portion of *Messiah*. Regardless of the expectations of the prophet Isaiah or of his hearers, Christians have interpreted the historical Jesus as the fulfillment of every element of the poem.

The poem is in the form of a birth announcement. A new age has dawned when "the people who walked in darkness have seen a great light" (Isa 9:2). An era of trouble and a feeling of abandonment have been replaced with a new sense of God's presence among God's people. The result is unrestrained joy and celebration like the people would experience at the time of a bountiful harvest or after an enemy had been defeated. And it is the decisive defeat of a military foe that is envisioned here. The bloody garments of the enemy are burned as fuel for their fire, as the yoke of oppression has been thrown off.

It is a natural human tendency of any person or group to read lyric poetry such as this through the lens of one's own experience. The people of Judah contemporary with Isaiah and Ahaz looked for a deliverer from the threats of Assyria, as well as Israel and Syria. Those living during the reign of Hezekiah who viewed his monarchy positively saw him as the fulfillment of this prophecy. The Jews living in exile hoped for another deliverer perhaps in the same mold as Hezekiah. The remnant living in Jerusalem during the first century CE no doubt thought of the Roman occupying force when they read of "the yoke of their burden, and the bar across their shoulders, the rod of their oppressor" (Isa 9:4) and continued to hope for a new champion. The disciples of Jesus came to see him as the fulfillment of that expectation (cf. Matt 16:13-19; Mark 8:27-29; Luke 9:18-20) although their understanding of Jesus' role and his understanding of it diverged sharply. Ensuing generations of Christians came to understand that Jesus was not interested in an earthly, political kingdom. Nevertheless, they saw his establishment of a reign in another dimension as the completion of the narrative begun by Isaiah centuries earlier.

The child whose birth is announced is not mentioned until verse 6, and even then there is no detail that would give a clue as to the identity of this heir to the throne. Instead he is given names that describe his actions. He is to be a "Wonderful Counselor." This denotes wisdom, possibly in contrast to the foolishness of Ahaz in seeking foreign alliances. "Mighty God" does not necessarily indicate divinity. Those who reigned in power were often referred to as gods. However, the operative word is "power." The people long for someone with the might to overthrow their conquerors, someone greater than the impressive armies that keep them in captivity. The "Everlasting Father" would look after the well-being of his children, the citizens of his monarchy. And the "Prince of Peace" would establish a time when the threat of foreign invaders was not a constant stress. He would be, in summary, the perfect king, the answer to the real and critical needs of the people.

In every generation and in any context of oppression or threat, these are the qualities that people in crisis look for in their leader. The biblical affirmation—in both the Old and New Testaments—is that this leader is never to be found perfectly embodied in any earthly ruler. Only Yahweh completely fits the description found in this unforgettable poetry.

The authority of this leader will expand and be limitless; it will be characterized by justice and righteousness; and it will be instigated and assured by the Lord of hosts. Is there any wonder that this poem has been read with hope, set to music, recited in worship, and seen as the summary of the aspirations of the people of God throughout history?

The Peaceful Kingdom

The remainder of Isaiah 9 and all of chapter 10 are a scathing indictment of the offenses of the northern kingdom (referred to here as Jacob and Israel). However, placed as it is in this period during the reign of Ahaz, it could easily be interpreted by the people of Judah as a bill of particular sins of which they were also guilty. It concludes with a reference once again to the "remnant of Israel and the survivors of Jacob" who will return not only to the land but also to their God (Isa 10:20-27). Isaiah sets both the condemnation and the hope in historical context by saying that the Lord tells them not to be afraid of the Assyrians because "in a very little while my indignation will come to an end, and my anger will be directed to their destruction" (10:25).

What follows (chapter 11) is a description of the kingdom that God will provide to those who have remained faithful. Characteristic of Isaiah, the terrible condemnations of the unfaithful are quickly followed by a message of future hope. Isaiah foretells the coming of a new Davidic king: "A shoot shall come out from the stock of Jesse" (11:1). As the kings in the line of David have been cut down because of their unfaithfulness to the covenant, now a sign of new life will come out of the stump. The initiation of this new reign is from God as "the spirit of the LORD shall rest upon him" (11:2).

1. In a time of great stress, Ahaz and the people of Judah sought help in unwise foreign alliances. When you are consumed by fear, where are you likely to turn instead of to God?

_____

_____

_____

_____

_____

2. Immanuel means "God with us." How do you see God as being with you in your daily life?

_____

_____

_____

_____

_____

3. What can you do to make the presence of God more real for you?

_____
_____
_____
_____
_____

4. What do you believe it means for Jesus to be the Messiah? How would you explain that to a non-Christian?

_____
_____
_____
_____
_____

5. What was the time in your life when you felt most vulnerable? How did you handle it?

_____
_____
_____
_____
_____

6. Our culture could be described as anything but "peaceful." What could we do to come closer to the ideal described in Isaiah 9?

_____
_____
_____
_____
_____

Warnings Unheeded

Isaiah 13, 14

Much of the remainder of First Isaiah, chapters 13 through 23, takes the form of particular prophecies addressed to the foreign nations that surrounded Israel and by whom they were often threatened. Oracles of this type appear in almost all of the prophetic books of the Old Testament. In each case, the nations to whom the prophecy is addressed are considered to be the enemies of Israel.

In the original Hebrew language in which these prophecies were collected, this type of writing is often introduced by the word *massá*, which means "burden" or "load." Scholars refer to these as "doom oracles." In holy wars of this historical period, a king or general would ask a prophet to pronounce a curse on an enemy against whom he was about to enter into battle. The oracles of Isaiah seem to fit this form although it certainly is not clear that Isaiah understood them to be curses against these nations. He was simply pronouncing the will of Yahweh relating to those who were enemies of the chosen people.

A classic example of these doom oracles is found in Numbers 23–24 in the story of Balak and Balaam. Following the forty years of wilderness wanderings and just before the death of Moses, the people of Israel were at the edge of the land of Moab. Balak, the leader of the Moabites, was fearful of the invaders and asked the prophet Balaam to curse the Israelites. Balaam was eager to please Balak, but he could only deliver the words that the Lord gave him and so, on three separate occasions, he ended up blessing the tribes of Israel instead of cursing them. Still wanting to please Balak, Balaam showed him how the Israelites could be enticed into sexual immorality with Moabite women, thereby cursing themselves. Although this picture is of a "prophet for hire," it is nonetheless consistent with the concept that any true prophet can only speak what Yahweh tells him to say.

In Isaiah's case, the oracles of doom are leveled against the nations that threaten the security of Israel and who eventually are involved in their defeat and captivity in Babylon. While the people, including the military and political leaders, are only able to see the immediate threat, the prophet points to the eventual doom of all who seek to thwart God's plan. While it was only natural that the people of Judah were most concerned with what was going to happen to *themselves*, Yahweh sees much farther down the historical road. As will be attested to near the end of the book of Isaiah (55:8), Yahweh's thoughts are not the people's thoughts and Yahweh's ways are not their ways. Nevertheless, through Isaiah God gives them a glimpse into the future.

The oracles collected in this section cover the entire span of the book. While some refer to events during the lifetime of the original Isaiah, others allude to the circumstances of the exile, or perhaps immediately after. Evidently, the final editors of what has become known as the book of Isaiah collected these doom oracles from different sources and included them in this section near the end of the time when the people of Judah lived in and around Jerusalem. Not all of these threats were immediate, but they demonstrate the tremendous stress under which Yahweh's people were living.

The political situation is similar to that faced by the modern state of Israel. A tiny nation, surrounded by enemies, Israel continues to face the temptation of depending on armed might as the solution of every threat to security. The roots of the unwillingness of the Israelis to negotiate or make peace with the surrounding states, many of which refuse to acknowledge the right of the state of Israel to exist, can be found in these ancient oracles.

The application of these texts to contemporary Christianity is not as immediately obvious. As members of the new covenant, we live in what is, for the church, a post-political age. That is, no particular nation can be identified as the people of God. There are Christians in virtually every nation on earth, so no clash of nations over territory or influence can be seen as meriting oracles of doom such as Isaiah issued. However, in many places around the world, governments, armies, and movements threaten the lives of Christians today. As an example, at the time of writing, many Christians have been driven from the Muslim world, especially in Iraq and Syria.

The additional application is found in the transient nature of these and all other regimes and powers. All of the nations to which the prophet refers are now part of ancient history. Kings and countries have come and gone. Many seemed to wield unstoppable power, but, in the end, all of them turned to dust. And throughout all of this history, the rise and fall of earthly powers, Yahweh stands supreme, the only unquenchable and undefeatable power.

The prophets who spoke for Yahweh throughout the book of Isaiah sought to remind the people of Israel of this one fact: the Lord shall reign forever.

Proclamation against Babylon

Babylon was the most powerful enemy that Israel faced. Many Jews came to regard this large neighbor to the east as "the very arch-foe" of the people of God (Kelley, 235). The regime was so oppressive of its neighbors that in the New Testament Babylon stood symbolically for Rome (see 1 Pet 5:13; Rev 14:8; 16:19; 17:5). Since in this oracle Babylon is the preeminent world power, this section has to be seen as part of the circumstances Israel faced in the sixth century BCE rather than during the time of the First Isaiah.

Babylon rose to ascendancy in 626 BCE with the defeat of the Assyrians. At the time the most powerful military power in the region, Babylon ruled all the ancient Middle East with an iron hand until it was conquered by Cyrus of Persia in 539. The thirteenth and fourteenth chapters of Isaiah appear to be from the time when Babylon was gaining strength.

The destruction of Babylon will occur on "the day of the LORD," a time when God will call out a mighty army from many nations to defeat the enemy of Israel. There is an apocalyptic feel to the description as the earth becomes desolate, the heavens tremble, and the earth is shaken out of its place (v. 13). On that day God will deal with sinners as the wicked, arrogant, and ruthless are destroyed.

In verses 17-22, Babylon is specifically designated as the nation to feel the wrath of Yahweh, and the Medes will be the agent through which God's will is realized. The Medes established a powerful kingdom in the seventh century in the northwestern part of what is now Iran. However, events did not go precisely as this passage anticipated. Both Babylon and the Medes were conquered by Cyrus of Persia. Nor was the destruction of Babylon as apocalyptic as described. Babylon actually surrendered peacefully to Cyrus and remained a thriving city throughout the Persian period. It was finally captured and destroyed by the Parthians in 127.

The fourteenth chapter is called a "taunt song." When the destruction foretold has come to pass, and Israel is free from the bonds of slavery, the roles will be reversed and Israel will be given rest. The song describes the death of a tyrant, although the specific ruler is not mentioned. The author may have been describing the eventual fate of any tyrannical ruler.

Scholars have divided the song into five verses or strophes. The first describes the joy that fills the earth when news arrives that the tyrant has died. Then the scene shifts to Sheol, the shadowy land of the dead, where the tyrant now resides and where he has no power whatsoever. He is welcomed by all the other former leaders of great powers on earth who are now just as impotent as he: "You too have become as weak as we are! You have become like us!" (v. 11). As this text is incorporated into the sacred writings of Israel, it serves as a reminder that all earthly kings ultimately fail. Though it may have been placed in the text well after the fact, it demonstrates that Israel's tendency to rely on foreign powers always resulted in a doomed alliance.

Then the poem describes the specific cause of the tyrant's downfall. It was pride that made the tyrant think he could be equal to God, but now that pride has been the source of his destruction: "You said in your heart, 'I will ascend to heaven; above the stars of God I will set my throne . . . ,' but you are brought down to Sheol, to the depths of the Pit" (Isa 14:13a, 15).

This picture of a ruler ascending and then falling may have been taken from a Canaanite story about a minor Canaanite deity who tried to sit among the gods and make himself like the one whom they called "the Most High." His pride led to him being cast not back to earth but to the depths of Sheol. The Canaanites probably drew this story from their observation of natural phenomena. Each day they saw the planet Venus rise in the east, only to be blotted out by the brilliance of the sun as it rose in the morning. They saw this as a cosmic reenactment of the contest between a minor deity and the highest god in their pantheon.

The prophet evidently took this ancient story and worked it into the taunt song because of its relevance for the people of Yahweh. Though they had been warned consistently to rely solely on the Lord for their protection, they made futile alliances with foreign powers in the hopes of staving off disaster. The end result was the very catastrophe they feared, complete domination and slavery.

This story was interpreted in an interesting way in the history of Christian biblical interpretation. The Latin translation of the Old Testament, the Vulgate, translated the name of the lesser god in the story as "Lucifer." Some early Christian commentators then connected this text with Luke 10:18 where, exulting in the return of the seventy disciples whom he has sent out, Jesus says, "I watched Satan fall from heaven like a flash of lightning." They saw this as a prehistory of Satan, the prince of demons. This interpretation was then picked up in Dante's *Inferno* and Milton's *Paradise Lost.* This is, however, as many scholars have noted, a misuse of this passage. As Kelley notes, "While the Old Testament takes sin seriously and comes to grips with the existential problem of evil, it is singularly free of any attempt to account for the origin of sin and evil, except perhaps in the story of Adam and Eve. To use this passage to pinpoint the origin of sin, therefore, is to misuse the Scriptures" (239).

The fourth verse of the poem moves back to earth where spectators stare at the body of the fallen tyrant. It is hard for them to believe that one who was so powerful has fallen so far: "How you are fallen from heaven, O Day Star, son of Dawn! How you are cut down to the ground, you who laid the nations low!" (Isa 14:12). Rather than receiving burial with the pomp and circumstance to which rulers were accustomed, he is thrown into a pit. This may have referred to the practice of hastily burying those who were killed in battle.

The final verse describes the legacy a fallen tyrant leaves behind. Ordinary people place a curse on the tyrant so that his children do not follow in his footsteps: "May the descendants of evildoers nevermore be named!" (v. 20b). Though he has displayed great power, nothing remains of all that he has built. The prophet includes this sad tale as if to say, thus it will always be to those who act as tyrants over people. Their pride will result in their destruction.

Though Isaiah applies this truth to the leaders of nations with whom the people of Judah are at war, the lesson applies to tyrants of any age. It may also apply to any individual who seeks to dominate another. A parent who takes pleasure in the humiliation of a child, a boss who lords it over employees for the sheer sake of showing his power, a spouse who demeans his or her partner—all of these eventually come to a bad end, and the tale of the fall of the tyrant in Isaiah 14 is a cautionary tale to all of them.

Additional Warning to the Nations

Following this extended pronouncement to the greatest power of the day, Babylon, are warnings against the other powers of the region, Assyria, Philistia, Moab, Ethiopia, and Egypt. These oracles can be summed up by a passage in the seventeenth chapter:

> Ah, the thunder of many peoples, they thunder like the thundering of the sea! Ah, the roar of nations, they roar like the roaring of mighty waters! The nations roar like the roaring of many waters, but he will rebuke them, and they will flee far away, chased like chaff on the mountains before the wind and whirling dust before the storm. At evening time, lo, terror! Before morning, they are no more! This is the portion of those who despoil us, and the lot of those who plunder us. (Isa 17:12-14)

Though the historical circumstances of each country may vary, their eventual fate is the same. This is particularly so if they seek to thwart the will of Yahweh by oppressing the chosen people. God may chasten God's children, but others are to leave them alone.

In the context of Israel's alliances with its neighbors, it is also a warning against the children of Yahweh placing their faith in any source of power other than their God. The prophet has warned them against dependence on any power but Yahweh. Their insistence on seeking help from their neighbors results in their eventual captivity in Babylon. As with the tyrant, their pride and naïve belief that God will bail them out of any situation, regardless of their rebellion, ends in disaster.

In chapter 24 there is an extended lament about the destruction that God's judgment will bring about. It is a result of the violation of the covenant between Yahweh and the chosen people. "The earth dries up and withers, the world languishes and withers; the heavens languish together with the earth. The earth lies polluted under its inhabitants; *for they have transgressed laws, violated the statutes, broken the everlasting covenant*" (24:4-5, my italics). Isaiah stresses again the tragedy that befalls God's people when they willingly choose to place their faith anywhere but in God.

Just one example of this dependence on foreign alliances is found in the thirtieth chapter. The people of Judah sent envoys to Egypt in order to arrange a treaty between the two countries. Jewish ambassadors carried expensive presents as an enticement for Egypt to align with Judah. Because at this point Egypt was under a competent pharaoh, Shabako, Judah believed they would be safe if they were on the same side.

The problem was that they had not consulted Yahweh. All important decisions of this type should have been delayed until they had received a clear word from the Lord. There is an instructive passage regarding this in 1 Kings 22. The kingdoms of Israel and Judah were allied in war against the Arameans. All the court prophets were telling the kings that victory would be theirs, but Jehoshaphat suspected that the prophets were only telling them what they wanted to hear. He asked Ahab, Israel's king, if there was another prophet who might be more honest. Ahab replied that there was one, Micaiah, but Ahab hated him "for he never prophesies anything favorable about me, but only disaster" (1 Kgs 22:8). When Micaiah did indeed prophesy disaster, Ahab had him thrown into prison until he returned from battle, but Ahab was mortally wounded while leading his troops. Trying to shut the mouth of the prophet did not keep his word from coming true.

It seems to be a part of human nature not to heed the warnings against our rebellion. We would rather believe that, through our own devices, we can make things turn out right, even when what we are doing is contrary to the will of God. The warnings of the prophets—from Micaiah to Isaiah—serve to remind us that this is the utmost folly.

The rest of the oracles of the First Isaiah deal with these warnings about seeking alliances with anyone other than Yahweh. The storm clouds of war with Babylon were gathering. The threat to the peace and security of Judah was very real. The opportunity to seek help from God was still available, but the rebellion of the people continued as they labored under the false belief that Yahweh would never allow them to be removed from the land of promise. Though the details of their defeat are not included in Isaiah's prophecy, by the time another prophet comes on the scene to pick up the story, Israel's defeat is complete and God's people languish in captivity.

1. In your lifetime, what powers have you seen emerge on the world stage, either regionally or globally? What has been the fate of each of those powers?

_____

_____

_____

_____

_____

2. In the "taunt poem" of chapter 14, pride is seen as the source of a ruler's downfall. How can pride cause the downfall of ordinary individuals too?

_____

_____

_____

_____

_____

3. How do Christians in the United States confuse the American citizenry with the people of God?

_____

_____

_____

_____

_____

4. While nations may look to other world powers for rescue, individuals often look to other sources to relieve the stresses in their lives. What are some of the sources of relief on which people rely, and, in each case, what are the limitations to the help they can provide?

_____

_____

_____

_____

_____

5. What are some of the biblical verses to which you turn to remind you that God is the ultimate source of your help?

_____

_____

_____

_____

_____

6. Can you think of times when you heard clear warnings about something you were doing that would displease God, but you refused to listen?

_____

_____

_____

_____

_____

A Message of Consolation

Session

Isaiah 40

Sometimes you ought to be able to see it coming. You're on a dangerous path, and any fool should be able to tell where it is headed. Abuse your body with drugs or alcohol, and eventually your body will give out on you. Constantly fill it with fatty, sugary food, and one day you're going to find yourself grabbing your chest or unable to walk or talk. Neglect your marriage, and, without even realizing how you got there, you'll be in some lawyer's office sitting across from your soon-to-be-ex spouse dividing up the family assets. Find a way to hide petty thefts from your employer until it develops into a habit of thievery that is no longer petty but eventually leads to disgrace and maybe even jail time. Focus your attention on your work to the detriment of your relationship with your kids, and they wind up wanting to have nothing to do with you. The paths are obvious and the results predictable. Sometimes you ought to be able to see it coming.

The story of the first portion of Isaiah raises this question: When the world *is about to* cave in, what then? The second section of the book deals with what often follows: When the world *has* caved in, *what then?* This is an account of a sad tale, repeated again and again throughout history, by nations and by individuals. Now, however, we are ready to hear the message of hope that follows the rebellion of the people of Judah.

When a person is on a path of personal destruction, engaging in conduct that can lead only to harm, sometimes there is someone who warns of the possible consequences. A person courageous enough to confront another with the reality of where certain behavior will lead tries to offer an invaluable service. Whether or not that warning is heeded cannot be the responsibility of the one who warns. The First Isaiah served such a role.

However, once those consequences have been brought to bear, words of warning and reminders of suffering are no longer sufficient or even needed. As suffering ensues and the reality dawns that this is a disaster of one's own making, then is the time for comfort and reminders of resources on which one can call. This task falls to the Second Isaiah. As the oracles of First Isaiah serve as a cautionary tale about counting too much on the patience of God in the face of rebellion and sinful conduct, Second Isaiah reminds us that the Lord is forever willing to provide help and comfort to those who call.

A New Beginning, a Different Age

We have come to an obvious and dramatic division in the collected works known as the book of Isaiah. Even without the benefit of knowing the Hebrew language, readers can detect changes in tone and expression indicating that time, location, and circumstances have changed. We have moved from the Jewish people living in their own land to subsisting as an exiled remnant. The political powers of the eighth century BCE—the southern kingdom of Israel, Assyria, Syria, and Egypt—have waned considerably in influence. Babylon is now the reigning superpower. However, a new power, Persia, is just offstage, waiting in the wings. And now the bearer of the message from God to this new environment is someone other than the one we have come to know as First Isaiah. The name of the prophet is never used again in the remainder of the book that bears his name.

The message has altered, although not completely, from stern warning about the consequences of sin to the hopeful message of comfort and the promise of return. Now the plea is that those in exile will trust God rather than Babylon. If they are ever to return to the land of promise, they must learn well the lessons taught through the negative example of their ancestors.

This movement from warning to consolation has been reenacted countless times throughout history, both in God's relationship with the chosen people and in human families. How many times have you seen a parent offer a stern warning to a child only to have to extend comfort when the warning has been ignored and consequences have ensued? Though the obvious temptation is to say, "I told you so," the immediate concern is that someone you deeply care about is hurting. The beautiful poetry that begins this section offers insight into the heart of Yahweh, who is a compassionate God even when the people have brought pain upon themselves.

From Uneasy Alliances to Exile

The oracles of the First Isaiah ended on a note of foreshadowing. King Hezekiah, who for the most part had been a responsible monarch, had recovered from a grave illness. King Merodachbaladan of Babylon sent envoys to Hezekiah to congratulate him on his recovery. As previously discussed, in Isaiah 39, King Hezekiah welcomed these envoys from Babylon to his kingdom and showed them all the treasures of his storehouse. When Isaiah heard this news, he offered his final recorded prediction: one day all of those treasures that Hezekiah displayed so proudly would be carried away to Babylon. Nothing would be left of Judah's glory, and some of Hezekiah's own sons would serve as eunuchs in the palace of the king of Babylon.

Less than two centuries later, all of those treasures did, in fact, belong to Nebuchadrezzar, the king of Babylon. They were the plunder of an invasion in 586 BCE. Beyond the loss of wealth, the far greater tragedy was that the elite of Israelite society had been carried into exile, the temple had been destroyed, and the people of Judah's faith in their God was shattered. All of the predictions of the First Isaiah—the futility of foreign alliances, the consequences of rebellion, the mistake of casually relying on the covenant with Yahweh—had come to pass. Were the First Isaiah alive to see these events, he would have taken no pleasure in the accuracy of his oracles, but he would at least have known that he had provided ample, though unheeded, warning.

While there is no accounting of this intervening history in the book of Isaiah, the Bible is not silent regarding this period. Second Kings 21 relates the disastrous reign of Manasseh, king of Judah following the death of Hezekiah. He ruled for fifty-five years, during which he reinstituted the worship of Baal and set up altars to many gods on the place where the temple had stood. According to the author of 2 Kings, the Lord's response to this idolatry was a verdict of stern judgment:

> I am bringing upon Jerusalem and Judah such evil that the ears of everyone who hears of it will tingle. I will stretch over Jerusalem the measuring line for Samaria, and the plummet for the house of Ahab; I will wipe Jerusalem as one wipes a dish, wiping it and

turning it upside down. I will cast off the remnant of my heritage, and give them into the hand of their enemies; they shall become a prey and a spoil to all their enemies, because they have done what is evil in my sight and have provoked me to anger, since the day their ancestors came out of Egypt, even to this day. (2 Kgs 21:12b-15)

This historical account of rebellion and consequence fulfills the expectation included in the message given to Isaiah at the time of his call. When Isaiah was informed that because of their rebellion the Lord would shut their ears and eyes to the point that they would be beyond immediate help, the prophet asked the obvious question: "How long, O LORD?" God answered, "Until cities lie waste without inhabitant, and houses without people, and the land is utterly desolate; until the LORD sends everyone far away, and vast is the emptiness in the midst of the land" (Isa 6:11-12).

These terrible results declared by Yahweh and foretold both by Isaiah and the author of Kings were set in motion with the disintegration of the Assyrian Empire and the rise of Babylon, led first by Nabopolassar and then by his son Nebuchadrezzar. Judah was invaded in 598, and in 587 Nebuchadrezzar left Jerusalem in ruins. Jews were scattered all over the Fertile Crescent, but the most influential concentration was in Babylon.

In this period of exile, a person or persons unknown took up the task of mediating between God and God's chosen people. Although the name "Isaiah" is never used after chapter 39, later editors bound the works of these two periods together, perhaps joining them with poetry from an even later period (Isa 56–66), under Isaiah's name to create a chronicle of God's dealings with the rebellious people of Israel and their eventual restoration. The story told by the First Isaiah, as powerful and revealing as it is, would not be complete without the details offered by the one whom scholars have come to call Deutero-Isaiah or the Second Isaiah. This new prophet accepts the calling to offer a message different in tone and content from that of the First Isaiah, but one that naturally follows from the heart of a loving God and that is consistent with the promises of future redemption found in First Isaiah.

For the modern reader, studying the book of Isaiah *as a whole* is critical to an understanding of the biblical view of God. Whereas the First Isaiah must warn stridently against the dangers of sin and the inevitability of its consequences, the author of chapters 40 through 55 is called to encourage people who are suffering those consequences.

Anyone reading today who is prone to despair over the mistakes of life and the results of rebellion is certain to find words of encouragement and hope throughout First Isaiah but also needs to move beyond the prevailing theme of judgment in chapters 1 through 39 in order to hear the much fuller treatment of hope and encouragement in the chapters that follow. Although written in different times for different audiences, these two works should be seen not only separately but also as a single piece. The people of Judah were carried into exile, but they were allowed through the providence of God to return home. God issued judgment against sin but was also the One who offered deliverance from the suffering that the judgment brought. Christians reading this text through chapters 1–55 see the picture of salvation history enacted through the old covenant in much the same way that Jesus brought those themes to bear in the establishment of the new covenant.

As Second Isaiah attests, "All we like sheep have gone astray; we have all turned to our own way, and the LORD has laid on him the iniquity of us all" (Isa 53:6). Those original disciples who professed Jesus as the Messiah, the fulfillment of the eschatological hopes of Israel, could not have avoided seeing the crucifixion of Jesus as the final and complete enactment of this prophecy.

What is played out on the stage of history in the chosen people of Judah is reenacted in the life of every believer who refuses to heed the warnings of the consequences of sin, suffers the inevitable result, and yet feels the loving call of the Creator to return home. Jesus described this relationship in an eloquent parable in the story of the Prodigal Son, more aptly called the Parable of the Waiting Father (Luke 15:11-32). The rebellious son, having suffered the consequences of his sins, finally returns home, expecting to be treated as no more than a hired servant, but instead he finds a father overjoyed at his safe return. The people of Yahweh living in exile should have counted on being treated by their God no better than the way the prodigal expected to be treated, and yet they too would find a waiting Parent, eager to welcome them home. Both Deutero-Isaiah and Jesus were seeking to convey the eagerness of Yahweh for the estrangement, whether of a person or a nation, or even of the whole world, to be at an end.

Instructions to the Prophet(s)

The new message of Deutero-Isaiah opens with orders given to the bearers of God's message to God's children in exile. (The instructions are in the form of a plural imperative, so God is commanding more than one person. Reminiscent of the scene in chapter 6 of Isaiah's call, the setting appears to be a heavenly court, with other beings present.) The words stand in stark contrast to God's angry response to the rebellion that led to the catastrophe of the exile: "Comfort, O comfort my people, says your God" (Isa 40:1). The stern warnings of the past are to be issued no longer. Israel has suffered enough. Like a parent who has allowed a child to suffer the consequences of her actions but cannot bear to see her hurt any longer, God sends the message that deliverance will come soon. This parental tone reinforces the relationship between God and God's people in exile.

The good news of the change in God's plan comes in three statements: "she has served her term," "her penalty is paid," and "she has received from the LORD's hand double for all her sins" (40:2). This last phrase does not mean that Israel has been punished to an extent out of proportion to her sins. Instead it refers to a legal requirement found in Exodus 22:3 that a guilty person had to restore double for crime (Childs, 297). Now God is saying, "Enough is enough."

This word for a new generation in exile is not, of course, the first time that the reader of Isaiah encounters God offering comfort to the people. Chapter 12, part of the beautiful poem regarding the peaceable kingdom, sounds this same note:

> You will say on that day: I will give thanks to you, O LORD, for though you were angry with me, your anger turned away, and you comforted me. Surely God is my salvation; I will trust, and will not be afraid, for the Lord GOD is my strength and my might; he has become my salvation. (Isa 12:1-2)

In the progression of the theme of God's relationship with the people of Judah, chapter 6 foretells the judgment to come, chapter 12 (among others) foretells the eventual deliverance, the period "between the two Isaiahs" recounted in 2 Kings and 2 Chronicles reveals the disobedience that results in judgment, and chapter 40 is a further promise of deliverance.

The Voice in the Wilderness

After the initial command from God, another voice takes up the refrain of change about to take place. A voice crying in the wilderness reveals that preparations will be made for the coming of the Lord. Highways will be made straight, valleys lifted up, mountains brought low, uneven ground leveled, and rough places smoothed. The writer is painting a metaphorical picture of the alteration of the political and theological scene. Mighty powers (interpreted by the exiles as the Babylonians) will be brought down while God uses other forces (soon to be seen in Cyrus of Persia) to bring glory to God. The exiles, rather than mere pawns in the struggle between military powers, are the witnesses to the action of their God, all brought about, according to the voice in the wilderness, in order to restore them to their land. Moreover, the return home will be a very public event. "All people shall see it together" (Isa 40:5b).

According to the author of the Gospel of John, it was the forerunner to Jesus, John the Baptist, who saw his mission either as a fulfillment of this prophecy or another example of it. When asked who he was, the Baptizer replied with an almost direct quote of Isaiah 40:3: "I am the voice of one crying out in the wilderness, 'Make straight the way of the Lord'" (John 1:23). Just as the original "voice" predicted a leveling that would alter the political landscape, John was proclaiming the ministry of Jesus that would turn upside down the understanding of righteousness and social standing, a world where "the last will be first and the first will be last" (Matt 20:16).

The return of the exiles to their home is the dominant theme of the Second Isaiah. In the increasingly mobile modern society, where many have been forcibly displaced from their homeland and other individuals have moved away from their roots, this homecoming should have particular appeal. Regardless of one's unfaithfulness, a loving God stands ready to forgive and to lead one home again.

A second voice now issues the command for prophetic speech: "Cry out!" (Isa 40:6). Another voice (presumably Second Isaiah) responds, "What shall I cry?" For anyone who has read the First Isaiah, the similarity to the call narrative in chapter 6 is immediate and unmistakable. A prophet is being asked to take up the mantle and speak the words given by Yahweh. The prophet protests that the people are like grass, temporary and unfaithful. His assessment is not very different from that of the First Isaiah: "I am a man of unclean lips and I live among a people of unclean lips" (6:5). However, he is told that "The word of our God will stand forever" (v. 8) and he is to lift up his voice with strength and declare, "Here is your God!" (v. 11).

Though foreign powers may seem to be dominant, though other gods may appear to have strength above Yahweh, though the chosen people may be humiliated and in exile, though hope may be gone, God is still there. A prophet or preacher of any age has the duty to proclaim to those in desperate situations, perhaps displaced or suffering the consequences of sin, that, all evidence to the contrary, God has not left the scene.

The prophet is twice called "herald of good tidings." Brueggemann notes that this "is the first intentional, self-conscious use of the term *gospel* in the Old Testament" (2:20). This opening poem is the great turning point in the corpus of Isaiah. All of the darkness and despair that are the result of rebellion, arrogance, and dependence on false gods are going to be dispelled, not because another foreign power more benevolent than Babylon is about to be ascendant but simply because "Here is your God."

It was tempting for the exiles to compare their God to the gods of those around them. After all, those who have depended on Marduk now lord it over them. Even before the display of power that would upend the political balance, however, Yahweh was proclaimed by the prophet to have no peer. The remainder Isaiah 40, beginning with verse 12, is a description of the works of God similar to that in Job 38. Just as Yahweh's speech to Job is intended to demonstrate that no creature is capable of conceiving of what God has created, so the speech in Isaiah makes the eloquent point that no being has done what God has done—nor has the power to do what God is about to do.

1. The beautiful poem that begins Second Isaiah portrays God's willingness to take back the chosen people after a period of suffering. Why do you think it is difficult to believe in the goodness of God when a person is very much aware of his or her sin?

_____

_____

_____

_____

_____

2. As you think about the events of your own life, when things "caved in," what did you do?

_____

_____

_____

_____

_____

3. Are there people in your life who tried to warn you when you seemed to be headed down a wrong path? Who comforted you when you realized your mistake?

_____

_____

_____

_____

_____

4. Have you benefited from a bad example, avoiding trouble because you have seen the consequences in the lives of others?

_____

_____

_____

_____

_____

5. Have there been times you were mad at God about something you were suffering, only to realize at some point that it was the result of your own action?

_____

_____

_____

_____

_____

A Message of Consolation

6. How is the history of Israel similar to the picture of God's relationship with individuals as Jesus portrayed it in the story of the Waiting Father (Luke 15:11-32)?

_____

_____

_____

_____

_____

7. Have you ever felt "far from home" because of something you did? Was your relationship with God, your family, or another person restored? If so, how did that come about?

_____

_____

_____

_____

_____

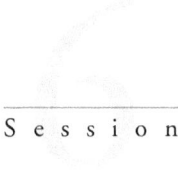

A Suffering Servant

Most of us understand the first rule of holes. When you have dug yourself into a hole so deep you cannot climb out, the first step is to stop digging! And the second step is almost always to call for help. It is the oft-repeated tale of humanity that individuals, groups, and nations end up in dire straits, unable to extricate themselves from crises. The crisis may be of one's own making, the inevitable consequence of bad decisions or sinful action. Just as often, the crisis is caused by external forces, powers beyond one's control. In either case, once one's own resources are exhausted and all avenues of escape are closed, one almost inevitably cries out for help.

For the children of Israel, who often found themselves both as a nation and as individuals in the midst of crisis, it was their natural practice to call on Yahweh to save them. The psalmist articulates this cry:

> Out of the depths I cry to you, O LORD. LORD, hear my voice!
> Let your ear be attentive to the voice of my supplications! . . .
> O Israel, hope in the LORD! For with the Lord there is steadfast
> love, and with him is great power to redeem. It is he who will
> redeem Israel from all its iniquities. (Ps 130:1-2, 7-8)

As Second Isaiah opens, Judah is under the domination of Babylon with many of its people living in exile, the direct outcome of their rebellion against Yahweh and their reliance on foreign powers that ultimately could not save them. They have no army, no international advocate, and no hope of human rescue. So now that they have come to the end of their collective rope, their reflexive response must have been to call out again to God for liberation. Perhaps the devout among them reminded the people of Yahweh's past interventions on their behalf and urged penitence and prayer.

Again the psalmist captures this mood of longing for former peace and prosperity in the land of promise:

> By the rivers of Babylon—there we sat down and there we wept when we remembered Zion. On the willows there we hung up our harps. For there our captors asked us for songs, and our tormentors asked us for mirth, saying, "Sing us one of the songs of Zion." How could we sing the LORD's song in a foreign land? If I forget you, O Jerusalem, let my right hand wither! Let my tongue cling to the roof of my mouth, if I do not remember you, if I do not set Jerusalem above my highest joy. (Ps 137:1-6)

In response to the cries we can safely assume went up daily, Yahweh sent word through a prophet in the tradition of Isaiah that the exiles would once again be redeemed. Just as God delivered the descendants of Joseph living in Egypt through the agency of Moses, so Yahweh would take decisive action to bring God's people back to the land of promise.

The first two chapters of this second section, 40–41, are a reaffirmation of Yahweh's willingness to redeem the chosen people. As had happened so many times in the past, most notably during the exodus, Yahweh chose to save the people from themselves, their oppressors, and the consequences of their rebellion. The long years of captivity and national humiliation were coming to an end. The instructions to the prophet are to "Speak tenderly to Jerusalem, and cry to her that she has served her term, that her penalty is paid, that she has received from the LORD's hand double for all her sins" (Isa 40:2).

However, in part of chapter 42 and in three other places in the remainder of the prophetic collection, there are poetic sections that indicate that their help would take a completely unexpected form. Rather than being embodied in a powerful, heroic military figure who would swoop down in almost magical fashion and rescue the remnant of Judah, as one might hope from a human perspective, the agent of redemption would be one known as "the Suffering Servant." Yahweh was indicating that the method of redemption would be through suffering and humiliation rather than triumph and exaltation.

If, in the midst of their own personal and national crises, the Israelites even heard this message of unexpected and unconventional rescue, you can imagine their disappointment. God was not going

Sessions with Isaiah

to send the conquering hero? If God had responded to their question through the prophet, the Second Isaiah might have said, "Well, yes, that will happen too. Cyrus of Persia fits your expectation of a hero. God will use him to conquer Babylon and eventually return you to the land of promise. But that is only the immediate means of extricating you from the mess in which you find yourselves. Your real redemption comes through the process of suffering and humiliation." This may not be the message that the exiles wanted to hear, but is this ever what we would want? Would this not be similar to the response one could expect to the invitation Jesus issued to his first potential followers: "If any want to become my followers, let them deny themselves and take up their cross and follow me" (Matt 16:24)?

The imparting of this message of triumph through suffering is to be found in four poetic sections interspersed through the remainder of Second Isaiah. It is not clear, however, whether they were part of the original oracle or a separate body of material later added by the editors (whoever they might have been) who collected the sayings of these prophets of Israel under the name of Isaiah. For our purposes, it doesn't really matter. As the later Israelites, now returned to their land, interpreted their history through the prophetic lens, the form and location in which we find these poems today is basically the same as they were received by the Jews in the centuries leading up to the Common Era.

The identity of the Suffering Servant through whom Israel will be saved continues to be much debated to the present day. The prophet, as spokesman for Yahweh, may have been indicating a specific historical individual, although no figure has emerged as a plausible redeemer. When you read the description of this servant, it stands in stark contrast to the powerful figure of Cyrus, so he could not be the one to whom it refers. Instead, the prophet may have been referring to the collective people of Israel as the agent through which Yahweh will demonstrate Yahweh's power. We might best keep in mind that we are dealing with the genre of poetry in these sections. As Paul Hanson puts it, "It seems in violation of the poetic tenor of the material to try to pin down the meaning of the Servant to one individual, one class, or for that matter, one time" (41).

Because there are several sections of Second Isaiah that refer to the figure of the Suffering Servant, it may be that there are multiple meanings. Following is a brief examination of each of those passages.

The Part that Israel Will Play (42:1-9)

Take a moment to review the contingent agreement discussed in session 1. The covenant relationship between Yahweh and the people of Israel was certainly not one of equality. God was understood to be the king, the undisputed sovereign who oversees the universe but takes particular interest in the chosen people. These select people, while "special" in terms of relationship, were clearly servants. Their ability to remain in their land and prosper depended on their obedience to their master. As the Israelites interpreted their own history, they did not see this as a forced relationship, but one into which they gladly entered.

In this light, the first of the Servant passages could be seen as a description of the role of Israel in Yahweh's redemptive plan. While their own condition in exile must have preoccupied their thoughts, now Yahweh informs them that they are to have a new mission. Through the covenant relationship between God and God's chosen people, God's nature and desire for relationship with all people will be both demonstrated and taught. Furthermore, this relationship will be most concerned with justice, particularly for the most vulnerable, the "bruised reeds and dimly burning wicks" (Isa 42:3).

Ponder for a moment what a dramatic reversal of human history this relationship depicts. While the world powers, including the ones with whom the Israelites were most familiar, the Babylonian and Assyrian empires, had used the brute force of military strength to achieve their goals, God was now using servanthood and humility for the accomplishment of divine ends. While world powers had destroyed enemies, leaving tremendous collateral damage among the most vulnerable of society, Yahweh's particular interest was in these who were without human advocates. In this situation, as always, God's heart is with the last, the lost, and the least.

In his commentary on this passage, Paul Hanson notes that the Servant is not a conqueror but a victim: "Is it possible that the reign of justice can be promoted by submission and the express renunciation of force, even by special attention and care to fellow victims who are on the edge of collapse and death?" (45). Thus, specifically identifying the Servant is not as important as understanding that he is to be the model for all who seek to follow Yahweh. They are not the ones who seek to dominate others but the ones who choose to serve.

There follows a poetic interpretation of the role of the Servant as "a covenant to the people, a light to the nations, to open the eyes that are blind, to bring out the prisoners from the dungeon, from the prison those who sit in darkness" (42:6b-7). This covenant has commonly been interpreted in one of two ways (Brueggemann, 2:44). One possibility is that Yahweh intends for Israel to live *evangelistically*, conducting themselves in such a way that others, even those outside the initial covenant relationship, are brought into connection with Yahweh, or that they are to *engage in social justice*, transforming social relationships so that the world is radically reordered.

These two possibilities have been either the twin emphases or the two options for any religious movement in its relationship with the world. Are the followers of God to be brought into personal relationship with the deity, or are the religious group members to seek to work for a better world, or are they to be engaged in both? In any case, in this specific context the people of Yahweh are to relate to the world from a servant mode. Rather than conquering opposition through power, they are to seek transformation through love.

Although the Servant, whether an individual or the people collectively, is given the mission, it is Yahweh who provides the power. Note the use of the first-person singular in the oracle: "*I* am the LORD, *I* have called you to righteousness, *I* have taken you by the hand and kept you; *I* have given you as a covenant to the people, a light to the nations . . . *I* am the LORD, that is *my* name; *my* glory *I* give to no other, nor *my* praise to idols" (42:6, 8, my italics). Readers of the New Testament will immediately recognize in this first Servant poem the connection with the calling of Jesus in the baptism in the Jordan. The author of the Gospel of Mark describes the Spirit descending from heaven like a dove and a voice proclaiming, "You are my Son, the Beloved; with you I am well pleased" (Mark 1:11). This ties the role of the Christ with the image of the Suffering Servant and the one in whom Yahweh delights. The author of the Gospel of Matthew quotes 42:1-2 directly in linking the healing ministry of Jesus to the understanding of God's chosen Servant.

These literary texts regarding the Suffering Servant stand in stark contrast to the actions of those, whether Jew or Christian or Muslim, who find their roots in the Hebrew narrative but who wage "holy war" as a way of fulfilling their calling to follow. Anyone seeking to be true to the calling of the God of Abraham, Isaac, Jacob, and Ishmael, and the Father of Jesus will take on the role of a servant.

God's Plan from the Beginning (49:1-6)

The second of the Servant Songs is placed in the mouth of the Servant himself. Although some believe it is impossible to pin down the identity of the one speaking (Brueggemann calls it "unfathomable," 2:109), verse 3 says, "You are my servant Israel," and this has been the traditional Jewish interpretation. The Reformer John Calvin, who generally interpreted the Old Testament allegorically, seeing the figure of Christ in many places, wrote regarding this poem, "This is spoken in the person of Christ, to assure the faithful that these promises should come to pass: for they were all made in him and in him would be performed" (Calvin, *Geneva Notes* on Isaiah 49:1).

The "third way" adopted by most Christian interpreters is to understand how the leaders of the early Christian church, as reflected in the Gospel writers, came to see the figure of the historical Jesus as the fulfillment of this role without claiming that this was the intent of either the original author or the editors who compiled the book of Isaiah.

Before the Servant was born, he was called and chosen by God. This is similar to the statement regarding the prophet Jeremiah: "Before I formed you in the womb I knew you, and before you were born I consecrated you; I appointed you a prophet to the nations" (Jer 1:5). As in the first poem, note that, though the Servant is the agent, Yahweh is the one who equips: "*He* made my mouth like a sharp sword, in the shadow of *his* hand he hid me; *he* made me a polished arrow, in *his* quiver he hid me away" (Isa 49:2, my italics).

The opening expression of the Servant's experience is bathed in the reality of frustrating ministry. He testifies, "I have labored in vain, I have spent my strength for nothing and vanity" (49:4a). Although separated by centuries, this could be the testimony of the First Isaiah, given the failure of the people and their leaders to heed his warning regarding their violation of the covenant. Throughout the book of Isaiah, there is this recurring theme of the lack of response to the word that comes from the Lord, yet there is again the reminder that the call to prophesy is from Yahweh: "Yet surely my cause is with the LORD, and my reward with my God" (49:4b). Through the centuries, the servants of God have been sustained by this awareness that, though the response may be negligible, the call is certain, the source is divine, and the reward is eternal. This conviction causes the determination that characterizes this and every prophet.

In verse 6 we learn, for the first time, the work of the Servant. It is to return and gather Israel, that is, to end exile and bring Israel home (v. 6). The homecoming had long been announced in chapters 40–48 and is to be made possible by the triumph of Cyrus. But it is the servant who will bring about the wonder of gathering. That has been Yahweh's mandate to the Servant, even prior to birth.

The second part of verse 6, however, may well be the turning point on which any further interpretation of the book of Isaiah depends. In fact, how the religious leaders of Judaism chose to apply this verse set the course for the future direction of Israel. Saving the remnant of Judah *alone* is "too light a thing" for the Servant. God has a larger mission in mind: "I will give you as a light to the nations, that my salvation may reach to the end of the earth" (49:6b). To the modern reader, this would seem to be a clear indication that the role of Servant was to carry the message of God's love to the whole world. If the people of Israel saw themselves collectively as the Servant, then through their suffering and humiliation the world would be brought to God.

This was not, however, the accepted Judaic interpretation. The religious leaders interpreted this passage, if they applied it at all, as meaning that they were to draw together the dispersed people of Judah. By the time of Jesus, the temple priests and Pharisees were teaching of the responsibility of bringing Jews together through residence in or pilgrimage to Jerusalem. Their understanding of the people of God had not broadened beyond the children of Abraham.

This stood in direct conflict with Jesus' direction to his disciples to carry the good news of salvation to the world. According to the book of Acts, when Jesus was about to ascend to heaven his disciples reflected the contemporary expectation of the Jewish people: "Lord, is this the time when you will restore the kingdom to Israel?" (Acts 1:6). Although these followers had spent approximately three years listening to Jesus teach about the universal application of the gospel, they still thought quite provincially. They may have seen Jesus in the role of the Suffering Servant, but if so, he was the Suffering Servant for the Jews. To this expectation Jesus responded, "You will be my witnesses in Jerusalem, and in all Judea and Samaria, *and to the ends of the earth*" (v. 8b, my italics). As Jesus interpreted his own role as that of the Suffering Servant, he was a "light to the nations."

In the earliest history of Christianity, the followers of Jesus sought to remain within their Jewish faith and tradition while maintaining that Jesus was the fulfillment of their messianic expectation. However, they were rejected by religious leaders, cast out of synagogues, and excluded from the temple. This was not for proclaiming Jesus as the Messiah. It was for claiming that Jesus was the Messiah *for the whole world.*

Humiliation and Vindication (50:4-11)

The third of the Servant Songs appears to be an abrupt insertion in the narrative that has little to do with what comes before or after. It is a reflection on the calling of the Servant of Yahweh who is to bring Israel home from exile. Now the specific vocation of the Servant is to be a teacher. In its immediate context, the remnant need instruction for their return and the Servant will provide it.

According to this poem, the Servant has been given a tongue that makes him credible and persuasive. He knows how to encourage and support the exiles. He has also been given an ear that allows him to listen to their plight. However, he is also abused, either by the Babylonians who don't want him to teach or by exiles who have compromised with their captors and don't want to be judged for their collaboration with the enemy. It is even possible that some reject his teaching because they have grown comfortable in their Babylonian life and don't want to go home.

As has always been the experience of the Israelites, however, the strength that the Servant needs comes from the Lord. Although he faces hostility, he will not give in. His stance is similar to that of the psalmist: "My help comes from the LORD, who made heaven and earth" (Ps 121:2). As if he were in a court, the Servant declares that Yahweh presides over the judicial procedure and will acquit him of any charges brought against him. Opponents have no power to indict, condemn, or punish. The Servant is completely grounded in the utter reliability of Yahweh.

Then the poem moves to a portrayal of what a serious worshiper of Yahweh may do. One is to fear, obey, walk, trust, and rely on. And all of this is to be done in spite of the unavoidable fact that they are living in exile. It will be the Servant's mission to direct the freeing of the exiles. However, if that is to happen they will have to move beyond their reliance on false gods and return to Yahweh.

Unfortunately for the Israelites, there is a negative response. The Servant reports that none fear or rely on God as they should. This indictment seems to apply to the whole community that is hesitant and reluctant to accept Yahweh's offer of homecoming.

Who could have seen *that* coming? After generations of living in exile, bondage, and servitude, now many of the Israelites apparently don't want to go home. Perhaps they have gotten so used to their life that they are afraid to change it. After all, they are dealing with a known situation. Going back home will involve struggle and, above all else, trust in God. For those who have lived in the land of lifeless idols for so long, such trust is not an easy thing to achieve.

The Life of the Servant (52:13–53:12)

The final Servant Poem is spoken by Yahweh, who is determined that the Servant will be honored and exalted. While a life of suffering and humiliation is described, the poem ends on a clear note of victory: "Therefore I will allot him a portion with the great" (Isa 53:12a). The poem offers a life story of the Servant from birth to death.

The followers of Jesus read this passage and quite naturally applied the description of someone who "was oppressed, and he was afflicted, yet he did not open his mouth; like a lamb that is led to the slaughter, and like a sheep that before its shearers is silent, so he did not open his mouth" (53:7) to their crucified leader. In the eighth chapter of the book of Acts, when Philip encounters the Ethiopian eunuch, the eunuch is reading this passage but does not understand to whom it applies. Luke, the author of Acts, says simply that at that point Philip proclaimed to him the good news about Jesus.

Thus, the Servant who had been seen either as a representative of the people of Judah or of some redeemer of those in captivity takes definitive form for Christians in Jesus of Nazareth.

1. As you read the passages related to the Suffering Servant, what characteristics or actions of Jesus came to mind?

_____

_____

_____

_____

_____

2. Can you think of examples of "suffering servants" today? What impact are they having on the world?

_____

_____

_____

_____

_____

3. In what ways does the church today function as a suffering servant for the world?

_____

_____

_____

_____

_____

4. Is the primary purpose of the church to engage in evangelism or to work for social justice?

_____

_____

_____

_____

_____

5. What activities, ministries, or programs in your church are designed to evangelize, and which ones help to bring about social justice?

_____

_____

_____

_____

_____

6. How have you become comfortable with the ways of the world so that it is difficult to put your trust in God?

_____

_____

_____

_____

_____

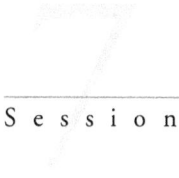

A Message of Salvation

Isaiah 41:8-13; 41:14-16; 43:1-7;
43:8-13; 44:1-5

What keeps a person from living a life of peace and purpose? If we are intended to live in relationship to God, as all of the prophets of the Isaiah literature clearly indicate, then why do so many people who seek to live spiritual lives appear to be unhappy? Second Isaiah addresses that question and offers the reassurance that such a life is not only possible; it is the life that Yahweh desires for all creation.

One of the greatest cripplers we face is fear. Whether we live a life of ease and security or a life of stress and chaos, fear robs us of the ability to act and to thrive. The exiles living in Babylon had many things to fear, most immediately the threats from their oppressors, but ultimately they feared God had abandoned them. If they had been carried off from the land of promise, then how could they trust that Yahweh continued to have any interest in them?

The prophet who had been told to comfort the people (Isa 40:1) is the conduit through which, again and again, Yahweh informs the exiles that they have not been abandoned; their God is still present, active, and planning their redemption.

Throughout Second Isaiah, the recurring theme is Yahweh's interest in the chosen people and willingness to take them back after their years of turmoil, separation, and exile. This message of hope and salvation is most often seen as applying to the children of Israel as a people. God deals with the nation, or the remnant of the nation, collectively. Through understanding God's relationship with the nation, individuals drew conclusions about their personal inter-action with their Creator. However, since at least the 1930s, biblical scholars have noted that there are some specific passages that take this message to a more personal level. The promise is not only of national redemption but also of individual salvation. These passages became known as "oracles of salvation."

In the long heritage of Judaic history that preceded the exile, individuals were the links that Yahweh used to communicate with people. Abraham, Moses, David—all of these heroes of faith were agents for God's relationship with the tribe. Now, through the oracle of Second Isaiah, God is offering a relationship with individuals regardless of the conduct of the tribe or the general attitude of the populace. The appeal is to personal faith. As much as the people needed to hear that they would be restored to the land of promise and that their enemies would be defeated, each person needed to know that God cared for him or her. They lived in constant turmoil and stress. Did the One with whom they once lived in covenant even take notice of them? Through the prophet, Yahweh gave a resounding "Yes!" to that question.

There are at least four of these "salvation oracles" interspersed in the prophetic word of the Second Isaiah tradition. They may simply be instances of the prophet turning from the theme of national redemption to personal application, as a preacher would move from general truth to personal relevance in a sermon, or these may originally have been separate literary compositions, placed by later editors at appropriate spots among the oracles to the nation. In either case, they are beautiful poems that testify to God's interest in the people of Judah as a whole and in each individual among the chosen.

Each of these songs comes in response to the recognition that, given the dire circumstances in which the people find themselves, doubt and despair are natural human reactions. This lament and response sequence is obviously not unique to Isaiah; it is found throughout the Hebrew Scriptures. The book of Lamentations, poems written after the destruction of the temple, is almost completely a collection of such cries of despair and expressions of doubt about whether Yahweh cares. Here is an example:

> Why have you forgotten us completely?
>   Why have you forsaken us these many days?
> Restore us to yourself, O LORD, that we may be restored;
>   renew our days as of old—
> unless you have utterly rejected us
>   and are angry with us beyond measure. (Lam 5:20-22)

In a similar manner, many of the psalms begin in lament but conclude with words of reassurance:

> Restore us again, O God of our salvation, and put away your indignation towards us. Will you be angry with us forever? Will you prolong your anger to all generations? Will you not revive us again, so that your people may rejoice in you? Show us your steadfast love, O LORD, and grant us your salvation. . . . Steadfast love and faithfulness will meet; righteousness and peace will kiss each other. Faithfulness will spring up from the ground, and righteousness will look down from the sky. The LORD will give what is good, and our land will yield its increase. Righteousness will go before him, and will make a path for his steps. (Ps 85:4-7, 10-13)

Following that same tradition, Second Isaiah (or some later editor of the prophetic material) interspersed similar promises of ultimate rescue within the larger dialogue of chapters 40–55. In a creative conflation of verses from some of these "salvation oracles," Philip Harner suggested a pattern for these passages:

(a) Fear not (44:2)
(b) O Jacob, my servant (44:2)
(c) for I am with you (41:10)
(d) I have redeemed you (43:1)
(e) I will not forget you. (49:15)

Taken together, these few words offer what everyone seeks: the knowledge that they are known, that they have not been forgotten, and that they will be cared for. The "salvation oracles" follow this basic pattern. Following are some of the passages generally considered to be part of this genre.

"Do Not Fear for I Am with You" (41:8-13)

One of the passages recognized as a "salvation oracle" is Isaiah 41:8-13. It is a stirring poem of assurance to people under the tremendous stress of oppression. If one is looking for the particular lament to which God offers the words of assurance in this song, this passage could easily be connected to 40:27: "Why do you say, O Jacob, and speak, O Israel, 'My way is hidden from the LORD, and my right is disregarded by my God?'" Notice how personal this lament is: "*my* way is hidden . . . *my* right is disregarded." This is more than national disgrace; this is personal crisis as well.

But then comes the response from the God who hears the call of God's people: "But you, Israel, my servant Jacob, whom I have chosen, the offspring of Abraham, my friend" (41:8). Yahweh joins these people seemingly disconnected from their heritage with the line of ancestors with whom, in the past, God has dealt in intimate and dramatic ways. Nevertheless, it must have been hard for the Israelites held in bondage, surrounded by foreign people and their gods and living far from home, to hear those words without an initial sense of irony. Where was the advantage in being the "chosen ones" if the result was their present misery? If they had given in to the temptation to worship foreign gods, it was not because they were impressed with the power of those human constructions but because they felt that their own God was so far away.

But then, after the initial address, the poem opens with stirring words of encouragement: "Do not fear, for *I* am with you, do not be afraid, for I am your God; *I* will strengthen you, *I* will help you, *I* will uphold you with my victorious right hand" (v. 10, my italics). Notice the first person singular pronoun. This is all God's doing. Christian readers of this passage immediately recognize these words set to music as the second verse of "How Firm a Foundation" and included in John Rippon's *Selection of Hymns* in 1787. For centuries, these poignant words of assurance have been sung in churches and repeated in the hearts of believers in times of stress to remind people that the One who was with Jacob and Abraham was with them as well.

All of Second Isaiah is a conversation between Yahweh and the people of Judah, carried on in the midst of chaos and stress, but in these salvation oracles God reminds them they have not been abandoned. They are encouraged to persevere and not lose hope, not because their immediate situation is going to improve but because the God who has been with their forebears promises to be with them as well.

These beautiful words of reassurance are not the last words of Second Isaiah. The people will continue to have to face the realities of bondage and oppression, but in the middle of this ongoing dialogue, these words come as welcome assurance of the presence of God. Yahweh cares for each of them.

While the book of Isaiah makes it clear that God's people have gotten themselves into their current predicament, the oracle also includes an acknowledgment that there are other human forces at work. Enemies who have been allowed by Yahweh's permissive will to oppress the people will eventually be defeated. "All who are incensed against you will be ashamed and disgraced; those who strive against you shall be as nothing and shall perish" (v. 11).

The simple but vitally important message of this song, "Do not fear," is carried over to the New Testament. At the birth of Jesus (Luke 2:10), the angel urges, "Do not be afraid; for see— I am bringing you good news of great joy for all the people." At the resurrection of Jesus, certainly a point of perplexity and confusion, the angel speaks to the disciples, "do not be afraid; I know that you are looking for Jesus who was crucified. He is not here; for he has been raised" (Matt 28:5). In the Incarnation, God was doing a "new thing" that could have caused as much uncertainty and fear as the exile had. God again sends forth the message: "Fear not."

"Do Not Fear for I Will Help You" (41:14-16)

Although the second salvation oracle follows immediately after the first, it has a very different tone. While the address of the first is to the "chosen," "the offspring of Abraham, my friend," this poem is directed to "you worm Jacob, you insect Israel." There can be no mistake about where these people stand in the hierarchy of creation! Brueggemann suggests that this may reflect the way the Israelites see themselves—"lowly, ignoble, without hope" (2:35). This places them in a posture of humility before "the LORD," "your Redeemer," "the Holy One of Israel" (v. 14b).

Despite their unworthiness, Yahweh will help them. The Lord intends to do great things through the people. The poem uses the metaphor of a threshing sledge, a farm implement that has the ability to sift and crush and refine the land in order to make it suitable for planting. God intends to use the people to make Judah inhabitable again while disposing of the enemy. And make no mistake: this is the Lord's doing. They are to rejoice not in what they have done, but "in the Holy One of Israel you shall glory" (v. 16).

These succinct verses contain a warning for all who are used by God for God's purposes. Like the children of Judah, they are chosen not for talent or ability or prowess, but simply because God chooses. Before the Lord of all creation we are all "worms and insects." And yet, through the providence of God we can be used to accomplish great things. Then the temptation is to believe that we have accomplished these tasks through our own abilities. This can never happen if we remember that without God we are nothing. It is to "the Holy One of Israel" that we must give the glory.

"Do Not Fear for I Have Redeemed You" (43:1-7)

Another of the salvation oracles addresses the issue of reluctant followers. It is one thing to be told that you will be taken from a terrible situation and restored to a place that your ancestors called home. It is another thing entirely to contemplate the trials you must undergo in order to get there. The oracle that begins chapter 43 anticipates those trials and offers assurance that no matter how treacherous the journey, the final result will be restoration. As in the first of these oracles, the primary exhortation is "fear not."

These can be inspirational words to people who recognize they have distanced themselves from God—are in exile in the far country—and who are afraid God will not help them as they make the long journey back to wholeness. As the prodigal in Luke 15 knew, it is hard to travel home when you are afraid that you will not be accepted there. However, just as the waiting father in Jesus' story did not allow his son to deliver his well-rehearsed speech about being willing to be accepted as a hired servant, but instead threw a party in his honor, Yahweh eagerly accepts all who will come back into the fold.

Before such a word of comfort can be offered, however, the people must be reminded of how they got into such a mess in the first place. The salvation oracle is set up by the verses that precede it in 42:21-25. Second Isaiah recalls for the people of Judah the fact that they have brought this disaster upon themselves. Because the people "robbed and plundered" (v. 22a), they were given up as spoil. "Was it not the LORD, against whom we have sinned, in whose ways they would not walk, and whose law they would not obey?" (v. 24b). There is a little "reality therapy" here that refuses to allow any denial that their crisis is of their own making. The disaster of exile was not the result of political forces that could not be overcome; it came about because God allowed their defeat due to their willful disobedience.

But then the voice of God interrupts this condemnation ("But now thus says the LORD") with the beautiful promise of restoration and protection. There is a dramatic change in tone. Whereas the prophet offers the word of accusation, Yahweh offers encouragement. As we have seen throughout the various phases of the Isaiah material, the action comes from God's side. These are not necessarily chastened people who have learned from their mistakes. As Brevard Childs notes, "The exile did not awaken Israel's conscience or prepare the grounds for a return. Rather a new word, solely from God's side wrought the change, opening the way to the future" (334).

The knowledge that God is with them is crucial when they consider the trials they will face going home. Even under the protection of Cyrus, they are going back to a desolate place. As they "pass through the waters" and "walk through fire," they will not be harmed because their God is with them. This is just the assurance they need— and that everyone needs in time of crisis. This is a word of assurance similar to that offered in the first oracle: they are not forgotten.

In verses 3-4, Yahweh offers to give Egypt, Ethiopia, and Seba as ransom to Babylon in exchange for Israel. This should not be taken too literally. The point is that Israel has a Savior who will pay any price to secure her freedom (Kelley, 310). It is similar to the profession of love that a person might offer to one deeply loved: "I would do anything in the world for you." Such is the love of Yahweh.

The final verses of the song (vv. 5-7) broaden the scope of Yahweh's interest in the people of Israel from those in Babylon to all the Jews of the Dispersion. God assures the people that those from the east and west and north and south will all be gathered together, "everyone who is called by my name, whom I created for my glory, whom I formed and made" (43:7). There were almost certainly exiles living in Babylon who had relatives spread through other parts of the world. They were reassured that they too were known by God and would be redeemed.

Walter Brueggemann writes that this section "articulates, as forcefully and compellingly as anywhere in the Bible, Yahweh's defining and uncompromising love for Israel, a commitment and devotion that completely repositions Israel's life in the world" (2:52). Such "songs of salvation" have been important to faithful followers of God in every age. In 1905, an African-American composer named Charles Albert Tindley wrote a hymn that echoed this desire for the certainty of God's presence in a troubled world. Even though slavery had been abolished in the United States, African Americans still faced terrible trials. Reminiscent of the Negro spirituals composed before the Civil War, it speaks of that same hope of God's presence recorded in Second Isaiah.

When the storms of life are raging,
Stand by me (stand by me);
When the storms of life are raging,
Stand by me (stand by me);

When the world is tossing me
Like a ship upon the sea,
Thou Who rulest wind and water,
Stand by me (stand by me).
When I'm growing old and feeble,
Stand by me (stand by me);
When I'm growing old and feeble,
Stand by me (stand by me);
When my life becomes a burden,
And I'm nearing chilly Jordan,
O Thou "Lily of the Valley,"
Stand by me (stand by me).

"Do Not Fear for I Will Pour Water on the Thirsty Land" (44:1-5)

What would the people of Judah face when they went home? Reports had reached the exiles that the land was desolate. Soil once fertile for the raising of crops and the feeding of animals had lain fallow for too long. There was so much to do when the remnant returned that it must have seemed overwhelmingly daunting.

More important, however, was that their souls were dry and thirsty too. The people had not only been away from their land; they had also felt separated from their God. Could there be a revival of spirit as well as territory?

In the face of such despair and skepticism, this oracle brings words of healing and reassurance. Yahweh, who formed them in the womb, was ready to help them. As in the other poems of this genre, the theme is "Do not fear" (v. 2) because God will "pour water on the thirsty land, and streams on the dry ground" (v. 3). It is a powerful metaphor not only for the demonstrable revival of the land given to their ancestors so many generations ago but also for the restoration of the Spirit of God within the chosen people. The poem pictures the land flourishing again like an oasis in the desert.

The result is not only a land that will sustain the people but also people who acknowledge their allegiance to their God. One will say "I am the LORD's" while another will be proud to have the name of the ancestor Jacob. Still another will write on his hand for all to see that he is "the LORD's." This is the beginning of a resurgence of pride, not in the nation but in their belonging to God.

Though most of those who read a book like this will not be living under any kind of physical oppression, we still find many reasons to fear. The threat of global terrorism, the damage we are doing to the planet, and the uncertainty of the world economy give any thinking person pause. A familiar phrase these days is, "If you think everything is just fine, then you don't fully understand the situation." Add to these global concerns the personally shaky ground on which so many people stand: fragile health, family stress, living on the verge on bankruptcy, and being either over-worked or under-employed.

For people paralyzed with fear, the need is the same as it was for the people of Judah living in exile and the residents of first-century Palestine: You are not forgotten. Your God still cares. Build your life on that firm foundation. The words of these poems resound through the centuries and can bring hope again to despairing people.

1. What do you do when you find yourself despairing? Are you likely to call on God only when all of your resources have failed, or is prayer your first response?

_____

_____

_____

_____

_____

2. Have you ever felt that someone didn't care for you, only to find out later that they really did? Have you ever felt that way about God?

_____

_____

_____

_____

_____

3. Are you uncomfortable "lamenting" the problems you face before God? Do you have trouble being honest about your feelings because you are afraid God may disapprove?

_____

_____

_____

_____

_____

4. What specific fears do you face? Are there reassurances in the "oracles of salvation" that could provide you comfort?

_____

_____

_____

_____

_____

5. Write your own "salvation song," including your hope for how God might take away your fears.

_____

_____

_____

_____

_____

A Difficult Return

Scripture, Christian history, and the personal testimonies of contemporary believers are full of stories of people who have rebelled against God but, through circumstances either dramatic or mundane, have felt the call to return and have responded. Almost none of those stories, however, have included an immediate and effortless return to spiritual and emotional health. Instead, they have involved accounts of tremendous struggle, lingering doubt, and repeated failures before finally restoration was accomplished. One such struggle is the story of the final section of the book of Isaiah.

We are about to turn to a third and final movement in the collected work known as the Prophecy of Isaiah. The second portion concluded with a stirring invitation to abundant life:

> Ho, everyone who thirsts, come to the waters; and you that have no money, come, buy and eat! Come, buy wine and milk without money and without price. . . . Seek the LORD while he may be found, call upon him while he is near; let the wicked forsake their way, and the unrighteous their thoughts; let them return to the LORD, that he may have mercy on them, and to our God, for he will abundantly pardon. (Isa 55:1, 6-7)

The Lord was opening the way not only for a return of the exiles to their land but also for a return to the covenant relationship under which their distant ancestors had thrived. Far from being the wrathful, angry God that they might have imagined, through the second prophet Isaiah Yahweh communicated to the exiles love and acceptance beyond anything they could have expected. Conveying such a message has always been the role of the prophet of Yahweh—to assure people that, though they have sinned grievously, their God is willing to take them back.

As the work of Second Isaiah reached this loving conclusion, historical forces were at work that would help to carry forth God's plan. After many generations of oppression and slavery, the Babylonian captivity came to an end. Cyrus of Persia defeated the Babylonians in 539 BCE. Beginning the next year, Cyrus allowed the people of Judah to begin returning to their homeland. The movement back into the promised land was most likely gradual, with other members of the Dispersion also returning home from other parts of the world. Many living in Babylon chose not to return, fearing the uncertainty of repatriation, but for those who exercised faith in Yahweh's continuing providence, this new situation called for a new body of literature, fresh oracles mediated by a prophet to the people of Judah.

In modern biblical scholarship, chapters 56 through 65 of Isaiah have been understood as that fresh body of literature, a third section of the work collectively called Isaiah. The concerns addressed in these final chapters appear to be those of returning exiles who face the formidable task of rebuilding a nation, a people, and a religious culture. This would place the writing between the return of the exiles in 538 BCE and the completion of the Second Temple in 515. This portion is usually referred to as Trito-Isaiah or Third Isaiah. There has been considerable debate about the authorship of this material, but there is no real consensus of opinion among biblical scholars. All we can say with certainty is that one or more prophetic voices take up the task of communicating God's message to God's people, now dealing with a postexilic situation.

The returning exiles were living out the promises of the first two sections of the prophetic corpus. In Isaiah 10, in a passage surrounded by condemnatory judgment and foretelling of the bleak exile that was about to begin, the First Isaiah proclaimed,

> On that day the remnant of Israel and the survivors of the house of Jacob will no more lean on the one who struck them, but will lean on the LORD, the Holy One of Israel, in truth. A remnant will return, the remnant of Jacob, to the mighty God. For though your people Israel were like the sand of the sea, only a remnant of them will return. Destruction is decreed, overflowing with righteousness. For the Lord GOD of hosts will make a full end, as decreed, in all the earth. (Isa 10:20-23)

So the Third Isaiah makes it clear that only a portion returning was part of God's plan. The Prophecy of Isaiah, taken as a whole, is crystal clear throughout that Yahweh is in control. The people of Judah are not simply the victims of historical forces beyond their control. Their exile is a result of their disobedience, but from the beginning it was God's intention to return some of the children of the rebellious Israelites to the land from which their ancestors had been expelled.

This theme of redemption is passed from one prophet to the next like the baton in a relay race. The main theme of Second Isaiah was this promise of return. The people of Judah had been reassured the temple would be rebuilt (44:28), that "your waste and your desolate places and your devastated land" would be teeming with inhabitants (49:19), and that other nations would "come over in chains and bow down to you" (45:14).

Unfortunately, the reality the exiles faced on their return was not so sublime. The historical sections in other Hebrew writings (Ezra, Haggai, and Nehemiah) paint a picture of inadequate resources and terrible living conditions. A lack of funds and opposition from neighbors forced a postponement in rebuilding the temple. Droughts, plagues, and hailstorms ruined the crops and left the people undernourished at the very time when all of their energy was required. Making matters worse, they were compelled to pay a yearly tribute to Persia and support the foreign soldiers who remained with them after their return.

The external problems were aggravated by political and religious infighting. Pictured in Third Isaiah are corrupt civil, religious, and judicial officials. There is simply no indication that the people who returned were chastened by their experience and were now ready to follow God sincerely. No different from our own generation, people were dividing into camps, falling generally into broad categories of liberals and conservatives. They fought over the interpretation of the Mosaic Law, the proper way to worship, the laws that needed to be enforced, the role of religion in society—all the while neglecting the needs of the last, the lost, and the least.

Adding to their difficulties was the question of what to do with the "foreigners" among them. While so many of the people of Judah were in Babylon, other ethnic groups from the area around Jerusalem had moved in, most of them without any connection to the original covenant. What was the expectation for their relationship to a society built so strongly around their religious faith? (Obviously, this continues to be a thorny issue for the modern State of Israel. As this paragraph was being written, political groups in Israel were seeking a stronger statement on the nature of Israel as a uniquely Jewish state. This underscored the conflict with the multitude of Palestinians who live within the country's borders. The problem of how to treat "foreigners" has not gone away.)

It was probably inevitable that, given their situation and remembering the promises of the prophets, the returnees began to doubt (again) the love of their God. The prophecy of Malachi begins with the words, "I have loved you, says the LORD. But you say, 'How have you loved us?'" (Mal 1:2). They were not seeing the providence of God at work in any way that they could recognize. It was the age-old question voiced to God, "But what have you done for me lately?" As the Third Isaiah expresses the frustration of the people, "We wait for light, and lo! there is darkness; and for brightness, but we walk in gloom" (Isa 59:9b).

The prophet Haggai, a contemporary of this period, diagnosed the problem very specifically. While they were facing the trials of reentering the land and beginning other projects, they had neglected the important work of rebuilding the temple. Haggai brought the word of the Lord to the returnees: "You have sown much, and harvested little; you eat, but you never have enough; you drink, but you never have your fill; you clothe yourselves, but no one is warm; and you that earn wages earn wages to put them in a bag with holes" (Hag 1:6). It is a picture of futility—and, according to Haggai, it was all brought about because they did not make the rebuilding of the temple a priority. This indictment was written in 520 BCE, almost two decades after the return had begun. It was high time the people turned their attention back to the center of their worship and the locus of their life together, the temple. This was not simply a problem of urban planning. It was a reflection of their unwillingness to acknowledge that their allegiance to God needed to be their first priority.

Most of what we find in Third Isaiah can be understood against this background of turmoil and the difficulty brought about by the refusal of the people to acknowledge that their first priority needed to be the worship of Yahweh. The two themes that resonate through this final section of the prophecy are God's intention to deliver them from their troubles and concern with how to rebuild the Jewish faith. It is a testimony to the patience and love of Yahweh that these tasks are even considered as possibilities. From Yahweh's point of view the possibility of reestablishing the covenant still stands, despite the ongoing doubt and faithlessness of the people.

Third Isaiah begins with the same *inconvenient truth* with which the entire book began. The covenant relationship between Yahweh and the people of Judah was *conditional*. Though they might never be completely abandoned by God (Second Isaiah had squelched that idea), their continued blessing depended on their adherence to God's law. The reminder of that truth comes at the very beginning of this third section: "Thus says the LORD: Maintain justice, and do what is right, for soon my salvation will come, and my deliverance be revealed" (56:1). Surely their history had taught them that relationship to the tribe was not enough. Right conduct was also required.

The work of Third Isaiah begins with instructions about conduct that give some indication of the challenges the returnees were facing and the disputes in which they were engaged. Then the central section is a series of lyrical poems that outline the promises Yahweh is making to the people. Finally, the third section moves back and forth between practical dealings with the disputes and the possibilities of the future. (See Brueggemann, 2:165–66.)

Emerging Disputes (Isaiah 56–59)

Before getting to the promises that are central to this final section, Third Isaiah outlines the disputes that made resettlement so difficult.

EXPANSION OF THE COVENANT (CH. 56)

God's view of the role of the Israelites in the world was far greater than their own. The Servant described in Second Isaiah had a role beyond bringing the people of Judah back into a right relationship to their God: "It is too light a thing that you should be my servant to raise up the tribes of Jacob and to restore the survivors of Israel; I will give you as a light to the nations, that my salvation may reach the ends of the earth" (Isa 49:6). The covenant with Israel was not *exclusive* but *exemplary*. Others who knew little of Abraham could come to God also.

One of the problems with feeling *chosen* is that it seems so special that one has a hard time believing others could be chosen too. The Jewish people traced their relationship with Yahweh through the blood of their ancestors. They were special because they were the biological descendants of Abraham, Isaac, and Jacob. In their collective understanding, they were not only covenantal people; they were *exclusively, uniquely* covenantal people. Their worldview would not allow for the possibility that God could look with favor on those who were not also children of Judah.

After the opening admonition to maintain justice, the writings of Third Isaiah continue with an effort to expand the Israelite worldview. Two groups tested the willingness of the Israelites to increase their vision of God's love. Were they to accept foreigners and eunuchs into the temple and thus into the life of the community?

The conservative position was to exclude anyone who was not of their race or who was physically mutilated from participation in the community. They were applying a strict interpretation of Deuteronomy 23:1-8. No one who had been sexually mutilated or was the product of an illicit union or who was a foreigner was to be allowed in the assembly. It was that simple.

The liberal position, of which Third Isaiah seems to be the spokesman, took a more open stance. Participation in the covenant community was to be based on action rather than heritage. The foreigner "joined to the LORD," and the eunuchs "who keep my Sabbaths, who choose the things that please me and hold fast my covenant" (56:3-4) have a name better than sons and daughters. The implied argument is that the Deuteronomic regulations had now been superseded. Now no one was to be denied entrance to the temple or membership in the community because of racial background or physical condition.

This teaching takes on practical application in the New Testament story of Philip and the Ethiopian eunuch (Acts 8:26-40). By the time of the early church, the conservative position had won out. When the Ethiopian had been in Jerusalem, if his physical condition were made known, he would no doubt have been excluded from the temple. This had not, however, kept him from reading from the prophecy of Isaiah. The passage he is reading is Isaiah 53:7-8, an account of the Suffering Servant who was like a sheep led to slaughter. When Philip joins the eunuch in his chariot, he interprets this as a reference to the Passion of Christ. Were the eunuch to keep reading, he would soon come to the opening of Third Isaiah that, rather than advocating his exclusion, argued that he should have been treated as a son. This small story is probably included by Luke in the book of Acts to emphasize one of his major themes: Christ came for all. This message of universal welcome seems to have been lost on many of the returning exiles.

This same inclusion applies to foreigners, proselytes who wished to convert to Judaism and who sought to follow the practices of the

Jewish culture. In one of the most universal statements to be found in the Old Testament (Kelley, 352), the Lord declares that his house will be "a house of prayer for all peoples" (Isa 56:7b).

This passage continues to have relevance as churches decide who will be allowed to be members. If the principles of Third Isaiah are applied, the doors must be open to any who earnestly seek a relationship with God. Heritage, prior conduct, or physical condition has no relevance.

PROPER WORSHIP (CH. 57–58)

The returnees faced two strong negative influences in seeking to reestablish worship in the temple and in the culture. One factor was the impact of superstition and magic. After the fall of Jerusalem, when there was no official place of worship, those who were left behind may have resorted to the native religions and pagan practices of their neighbors. The battle against idolatry was not finished with the exodus from Babylon.

The other influence was the hyper-fundamentalism that would eventually result in Pharisaism. Religious leaders, both priests and laity, became overly concerned with the exact practices of worship and precise application of Mosaic laws without consideration of the higher good of how one treats others. Much as the First Isaiah railed against the practices of those who trampled the Lord's courts and "held solemn assemblies with iniquity" (1:12-13), Third Isaiah condemned those who "fast but do not see," who "serve your own interest on your fast-day, and oppress all your workers" (58:3).

Yahweh speaks to connect true worship with ethical action:

> Is not this the fast that I choose: to loose the bonds of injustice, to undo the thongs of the yoke, to let the oppressed go free, and to break every yoke? Is it not to share your bread with the hungry, and bring the homeless poor into your house; when you see the naked, to cover them, and not to hide yourself from your own kin? (Isa 58:6).

The passage foreshadows the parable that Jesus tells in Matthew 25:31-46, where those who are counted among the faithful are those who gave food to the hungry, drink to the thirsty, clothing to the naked, and presence to the sick and imprisoned.

Modern readers of this third section can find themselves under the same scrutiny. Do we focus attention and energy on the externals of how we worship rather than on whether we are putting the truths we learn in worship into practice? Do we debate with others the proper mode of baptism or the meaning of the Lord's Supper without letting those central ordinances draw godly lives out of us?

CONTINUING INJUSTICE AND OPPRESSION (CH. 59)

Apparently the people of Judah were using the courts to their own advantage, oppressing others by application of the law, often by distorting its meaning. As Walter Brueggemann observes, "When the courtroom is distorted by lies and misrepresentation, no one is safe" (2:196). Third Isaiah brings the indictment: "No one brings suit justly, no one goes to law honestly; they rely on empty pleas, they speak lies, conceiving mischief and begetting iniquity" (59:4).

The people were complaining that God had abandoned them, yet a close relationship with Yahweh may have been the last thing they really desired. A close relationship places one's life under the scrutiny of divine power, and for the Israelites that could only mean that their unjust practices, using the law not for the common good but to oppress others, would have to come to light.

All of these issues, taken together, paint a picture of people who said they wanted God to be present in their lives again but who were not willing to live in ways that would merit God's favor. Another faithful prophet brought to the forefront once again the *inconvenient truth* that they were not truly seeking a covenantal relationship.

The Promises of God (Isaiah 60–62)

Fortunately, the collected works of Isaiah do not end on that bleak note of disobedience and continuing struggle. The heart of this final section, chapters 60–62, is far more optimistic and hopeful. Brueggemann finds in this section "an unqualified and undisputed buoyancy about the future" (2:203). Hanson speculates that this section was actually written earlier in the period of return than the previous section but placed here to demonstrate an ongoing belief in God's promises (2:217-218). Despite the ongoing disobedience of the returnees, Yahweh remains faithful.

In this section, God speaks to the pessimism that must have been growing as the exiles slowly trickled back into the land, as attempts to rebuild the temple got lost in more immediate concerns, as partisan bickering developed, and as poverty and want became "the new normal." How were the people to maintain faith in God when evidence at hand seemed to indicate that they were still on their own?

The poetry of these three chapters might be dismissed as empty-headed optimism, a Pollyanna approach to life that keeps believing things are going to get better, even when all evidence points to the contrary. However, these poems clearly reflect an awareness of the negative circumstances under which people are living and challenge them to rise above their problems. The opening lines are a call to action: "Arise, shine; for your light has come, and the glory of the LORD has risen upon you" (Isa 60:1). As Hanson expresses this theme, "It is obvious that the prophet presented as the introduction to a composition that was intended to renew the hope of a wavering community an image timeless in its majesty and power" (220).

In times of great stress, there are two options: face the problems or look for the source of help. Readers of the New Testament might be reminded of the story of Jesus walking on the sea (Matt 14:22-33). Jesus' disciples had been in a small boat all night, battling a head-wind. They were dealing with the problem at hand, keeping their boat afloat, when they saw Jesus walking on the lake. At first they were frightened, thinking he was a ghost. When you are already in trouble it is easy to think the worst. However, Jesus reassured them, "Take heart, it is I; do not be afraid" (v. 27). This is the message of Yahweh to the returning exiles. Their God is with them, regardless of the darkness that surrounds them.

In Matthew's account Peter impetuously jumped out of the boat and headed toward Jesus. Perhaps the central meaning of the story—and the reason Matthew includes it—is found in the fact that, as long as Peter kept his eyes on Jesus he too could walk on water, but the moment he looked down at the waves he began to sink. Similarly, when the children of Judah focused on the seemingly insurmountable difficulties that beset them, they were overwhelmed. These poems reminded them to look to the source of their strength: "The sun shall no longer be your light by day, nor for brightness shall the moon give light to you by night; but the LORD will be your ever-lasting light, and your God will be your glory. . . . I am the LORD; in its time I will accomplish it quickly" (Isa 60:19, 22b).

Since this promise was not seen as having been accomplished with the return of the exiles, the children of Judah continued to look for its future fulfillment. They still awaited their messiah. Isaiah 61 is a poem written in the first person singular announcing what this messiah would be like. He would be anointed by the Lord to preach the good news to the oppressed, broken-hearted, and captives, and to proclaim the year of Jubilee, a time when slaves would be set free. While Jesus would appropriate those verses for himself a few generations later, the exiles sought the more immediate relief of someone coming to restore Israel to its former glory. While they might no longer be captives in Babylon, their plight is still so serious they will never be able to escape it on their own. Someone must show them the way.

This would be the basis of one messianic expectation at the time of the inauguration of Jesus' ministry. When Jesus read this passage in Nazareth (Luke 4:18-19), it was quite natural for some to be looking for a deliverer who would throw off the bonds of Roman domination just as Cyrus had defeated the Babylonians. This was not, of course, the path that Jesus chose, instead asserting that his "kingdom is not of this world" (John 18:36).

This central section concludes with the assurance that the One who was seeking them has not given them up. Although the people are no longer in captivity, it appears that the land is withholding its blessing, and their only conclusion is that God has abandoned them. This poem makes it clear, though, that nothing could be further from the truth. God has redeemed them whenever they have sought redemption; all that is required now is absolute repentance. The people plead to God, "Turn back for the sake of your servants, for the sake of the tribes that are your heritage" (Isa 63:17).

A New Heaven and a New Earth (ch. 63-66)

The heart of Third Isaiah is lofty and poetic. The last few chapters, however, get down to specifics about God's retribution toward former enemies and the restoration of Jerusalem. God comes as a mighty warrior who will exact vengeance against those who have oppressed Israel. The writer is confident that God will be victorious over their enemies.

The remainder of the book comprises a summary outline of all that has taken place in Yahweh's dealings with the children of Judah. The people are urged to remember the days of old when God was gracious to them. Then, however, their sin caused the rift that had brought such suffering. Now the prophet pleads for a renewed sense of God's presence:

> O that you would tear open the heavens and come down, so that
> the mountains would quake at your presence—as when the fire

kindles brushwood and the fire causes water to boil—to make your name known to your adversaries, so that the nations might tremble at your presence! When you did awesome deeds that we did not expect, you came down, the mountains quaked at your presence. From ages past no one has heard, no ear has perceived, no eye has seen any God besides you, who works for those who wait for him. (Isa 64:1-4)

As much as those who lived in Israel before the exile needed it, as much as the people living in captivity longed for it, now the returned exiles plead for an awareness of God's presence among them. And yet the magnificent prophetic work known as the book of Isaiah concludes with the people still not fully in the covenantal relationship that God desired. Far too soon they would experience foreign domination once again, this time from the Romans, and again waiting a deliverer. It was to take five centuries for the fulfillment of prophecies of a Suffering Servant who would take upon himself the sins of the people.

1. If you have ever found yourself in a difficult crisis and asked God to help you, what were some of the painful steps necessary for restoration and healing?

_____

_____

_____

_____

_____

2. Have you ever expected God to deliver you in a particular way, only to find that God dealt with you in a completely different way? What has that taught you about faith?

_____

_____

_____

_____

_____

A Difficult Return

3. When you face a tough situation, are you more likely to concentrate on the difficulties you face, the obstacles that must be overcome, or the divine power that is available to help you?

_____
_____
_____
_____
_____

4. When the Israelites returned to the land of promise, they quickly devolved into camps of liberals and conservatives on many issues. Do you believe such labels are helpful? Why or why not?

_____
_____
_____
_____
_____

5. Consider the issues we face in our culture today. Where do you see God asking you to take a stand?

_____
_____
_____
_____
_____

6. The Israelites had to consider how to relate to the "foreigners" who were now living in the land they called their own. What do you consider to be your responsibility as a follower of God in relating to the people around you who are not part of your religious heritage?

_____
_____
_____
_____
_____

7. As was true in First Isaiah, the practice of worship was an indication of how the Israelites focused on external practice rather than inward righteousness. In what ways do you see that happening in worship today?

_____

_____

_____

_____

_____

A Christian Reading of Isaiah

Isaiah 61:1-7

How is a Christian to read a work like the book of Isaiah? As one of the sixty-six books of the Christian canon, it is considered to be Holy Scripture, but how does one read this book *specifically?* We should always keep in mind that Isaiah and the other books that we call collectively the Old Testament were Hebrew Scripture long before they became part of the Christian Bible, but as Christians it is virtually impossible to read Isaiah except through the lens of Christian teaching, experience, and history. Given this prior knowledge and perspective, what approaches are available to us?

A Work of History

The text we know as the book of Isaiah was written over a period of several centuries, in varying but specific historical contexts, and by three or perhaps more people used by God to speak to God's people. Eventually a person or persons unknown collected these disparate sets of writings into what we now have as a single book. As editors always do, these people made choices. They may have had other material at their disposal that they chose to leave out. They had to decide the order in which they would include each piece. They made critical judgments regarding the authentic nature of some parts of what they had. Even this editing process itself probably did not take place during a single era, but developed over time until the book took the form that we have today. Through this process, a document resulted that tells us a great deal about the history of Israel in the eighth through the fifth centuries BCE.

Although we may gain historical insight from the final composition, these editors were not seeking to compile a work of history, *per se.* Reading Isaiah from beginning to end—from eighth-century children of Abraham living in Judea in the midst of a political crisis through decades of exile in Babylon through the earliest days of return to the promised land—one gets a sense that the editors were reflecting the interests of the original prophets. They were not seeking to give an account of history but to demonstrate God's activity within history, and specifically within the history of the people of Judah.

Does God intervene in human history? The book of Isaiah answers with a resounding "Yes!" The prophets that we have called by the collective name Isaiah spoke God's word not so much about *what people should do* but about *what God was doing.* God was holding the people of Judah accountable for their treatment of the poor and powerless among them. God was passing judgment on their inauthentic and hypocritical approach to worship. God was directing the forces of armies to lead them out of the land that they believed was theirs by right of birth. God was the one who stood by them during those long years of captivity, even when they felt that they were abandoned. God chose to allow Cyrus to defeat the Babylonians so that the chosen people might go home. And when their lives as returning exiles was not what they dreamed it would be, it was God who demanded that they refocus their priorities on building the temple and restoring proper worship rather than dedicating their efforts to their own interests. God as revealed through the writings of the prophets collectively known as Isaiah is an active, historically involved deity who directs political and military forces as well as the members of a tribe and the lives of individuals.

For the Christian, reading this ancient story raises questions about subsequent history. Was God only interested in history as it related to the Israelites, or were they truly to be a "light to the nations," demonstrating how God works in all of history? Are people still held accountable by God for their treatment of others, the nature of their worship, their devotion to God, and their refusal to accept the idols of their culture? Even when nations do not see themselves as "chosen," do those in power, as well as ordinary citizens, have responsibilities related to their treatment of people? If one accepts Isaiah as Scripture, then its teachings continue to have relevance for those who enter into the new covenant as much as they did for those in the old.

A Cautionary Tale

One of the ways to read Isaiah is as a series of lessons about how *not* to be the followers of God. While some of the oracles were addressed to the tribe, others dealt with individual conduct. Truths can be drawn from both types that help us to lead lives closer to God.

It is a tenet of Christian faith that God does not only deal with nations and tribes. The Incarnation reveals that God is interested in the life of each individual, and through faith in Christ a person enters into a covenant relationship. While God as revealed through Isaiah related primarily to the tribe, God as revealed through Jesus relates to individuals. Each person decides for himself or herself whether or not to enter into that relationship. As was true in the case of the Israelites, however, the covenant is always contingent on proper conduct. There are lessons for individuals in the story of the children of Judah.

Christians need to remember that *the covenant with God continues to be a contingent agreement.* While ultimately salvation is a gift that cannot be earned, the ongoing experience of God's favor on one's life depends on living a life pleasing to God. The children of Judah took for granted that divine blessing was their right by birth. It took defeat and exile to demonstrate that this was a terrible fallacy. Willful disobedience leads to estrangement. Glibly asserting that faith in Christ means one has "his ticket punched" for heaven does not mean that being blessed by God is guaranteed. Now, as in the time of the prophets, favor is still found in doing the will of God.

Idolatry continues to be an issue that plagues the people of God. Most Christians today are too sophisticated to believe that there is power in a wood or metal statue made by human hands. However, an idol can be anything that has a higher priority in one's life than devotion to God. Obsessive consumerism, a lust for power, worshiping of the flesh, a near-suicidal devotion to work, and even an inordinate bowing to the wishes of one's family can take the place of full allegiance and devotion to God. This is the type of idolatry that Isaiah warned against. Nothing short of complete allegiance to the God who declared, "You shall have no other gods before me . . . for I the LORD your God am a jealous God" will suffice (Exod 20:3, 5c). Reading the account of the idolatry of the children of Judah reminds us that even in a culture where godly worship is endorsed, it is easy to be lured into devotion to false deities.

Closely tied to idolatry is *a reliance on any source of ultimate strength other than God.* When the people of Judah, and especially their rulers, felt threatened by the military force of their neighbors, rather than remaining independent from foreign armies and staying under God's protection, they sought alliances with the countries that they assumed to be predominant. Ultimately these forces proved inadequate for staving off the power of the Babylonians. God allowed many of them to be carried into captivity not because they had backed the losing side in territorial wars, but because they had sought help from any force other than the Almighty.

Christians may seek protection from some source other than the ultimate. Modern followers of God may believe in a strong military for the simple reason that it makes them feel more secure, regardless of whether or not the army is used in an ethical way. On a more personal level, people may seek to protect themselves by acquiring as much money as possible in the belief that this will ultimately keep them from harm. For still others, when life appears overwhelming, rather than seeking the help of God to deal with the storms of life, they may seek solace in alcohol or drugs, numbing themselves to realities they do not wish to face. When life is caving in, where does one go for help? Christians, as much as the children of Judah, should reflect the words of Psalm 121:1-2: "I lift up my eyes to the hills— from where will my help come? My help comes from the LORD, who made heaven and earth."

Insincere worship may be as much a tendency for Christians attending services in modern buildings as it was for the people of Jerusalem who entered the first temple. God is no more impressed with meaningless ritual today than when Isaiah recorded, "What to me is the multitude of your sacrifices? says the LORD . . . . When you come to appear before me, who asked this from your hand? Trample my courts no more" (Isa 1:11a, 12).

In the oracles of the First Isaiah, proper worship and ethical conduct are closely joined. Unless worship elicits right action, it is meaningless. We are enjoined, "Wash yourselves; make yourselves clean; remove the evil of your doings from before my eyes; cease to do evil, learn to do good; seek justice, rescue the oppressed, defend the orphan, plead for the widow" (1:16-17). Today there is a great deal of creative ferment around the topic of how to make worship "relevant," but relevance is demonstrated by the subsequent conduct of the worshipers.

This conduct is most critical in our treatment of others. In our age of great economic disparity, *failure to protect the powerless* is still an issue. When Isaiah spoke of the oppressed, the orphan, and the widow, he was listing representatives of groups incapable of caring for themselves without the help of the more fortunate, and, on behalf of Yahweh, he severely castigated those who thought they were excused from the duty of caring for any but their own. Jesus identified similar groups when he spoke of the hungry, thirsty, naked, sick, and imprisoned (Matt 25:31ff), concluding that those who did not demonstrate their faith through care of "the least of these" would "go away into eternal punishment" (v. 46). Anyone who ignores the responsibility for ethical treatment of others by asserting that he is saved by grace alone should find the reading of the prophecies of Isaiah deeply disturbing.

The *result of the rebellion* of the people of Judah also serves as a cautionary tale. The story of God's dealing with the people of the covenant is one of extreme—but not unlimited—patience. After repeated warnings about the potential consequences of their sin, the conclusion of First Isaiah is that God drove the people out of the land of promise and sent many into exile as punishment for their rebellion.

Modern people resist any appeal based on the threat of punishment, especially eternal punishment. Many Christians are repulsed by a negative approach to faith. They may properly assert that God is first and foremost a God of love, a God who demonstrates patience and a willingness to accept back into the fold any who will come. The word of caution injected by the saga of the people of Judah, however, is that time eventually runs out, even on the patience of God. As early as the calling of the first Isaiah, the message was that God was hardening the hearts of the people so that they would not listen. This is not meanness on God's part but a recognition that if they intended to heed the commandments, they would have done so already.

A reliance on God's never-withdrawing acceptance fails to take into account the story told in the book of Isaiah and, more important, the gift of independence that God has granted to each individual. The Apostle Paul wrote that even those who were not part of the covenant should have known to obey God by natural law, but when they refused, "God gave them up in the lusts of their hearts to impurity" (Rom 1:24). People immersed in Christian culture have even less of an excuse. Despite seemingly endless entreaties, God eventually accepts one's decision to go one's own way.

Another lesson from Isaiah is the challenge to *the assumption that success is always achieved through victory.* When the Israelites were settling into the promised land and forming the nation that eventually became the kingdom of David, they achieved success at the expense of the people already living in the land. They came to see their military victories and their subsequent prosperity as signs of God's favor. They might have been able to see their defeats as signs of God's displeasure, but they continued to believe that if they repented their fortunes would be restored. On that basis, the exiles looked for a redeemer who would act as God's agent in reclaiming former glory.

For that reason, the oracles of the Second Isaiah related to a Suffering Servant must have come as quite a shock. It was hard for them to believe that God's will could be achieved and demonstrated through one who would be defeated. Biblical scholars today believe that the Suffering Servant, at least in the original context, referred to the exiles themselves. God was demonstrating power through their defeat and through the critical truth that they were not abandoned or bereft of hope, even in their darkest hours.

The writers of the New Testament Gospels portray Jesus as taking upon himself that same role, showing the power of God through servanthood, death, and what appeared to be defeat but was ultimately God's victory. Like the people of Judah, the disciples of Jesus looked for a victory that could be interpreted in human terms. Even after the resurrection, they asked him, "Lord, is this the time when you will restore the kingdom to Israel?" (Acts 1:6b). Even after the crucifixion and the triumph over the grave, they still assumed that success would be measured in earthly terms.

The modern "prosperity gospel" that asserts that God wants God's people to gain success and attain worldly goods is a descendant of this type of thinking. Even those who don't believe that God intends for us to have every material blessing sometimes speculate out loud about why God is punishing them if life does not go as they hoped it would. The model of the suffering servant reminds us that our own role is not to be a conquering hero but a servant of others who may have to suffer for our godly actions. Rather than being a sign of God's displeasure, suffering as a result of servanthood is evidence that we are on the right path.

Nevertheless, in times of crisis, whether the result of following God's will, because of our own foolish actions, or simply through misfortune, we, like the ancient children of Judah, need to know that we have not been abandoned by God. When the First Isaiah sought to assure King Ahaz that God was with them as opposing forces gathered around him, the prophet foretold that a woman who was already pregnant would bear a son and his name would be Immanuel, which means "God is with us." There is no further reference in Isaiah to a specific child by that name, but during that crisis they were assured

God was there. During the exile this message was needed even more, and so the second section of the book opens with the exhortation to the prophet to comfort God's people.

The Christian's mind immediately moves from the seventh chapter of Isaiah, the dialogue between the prophet and Ahaz, to the opening of the Gospel of Matthew, where Joseph receives word from an angel that Mary will have a son. He is told that the boy is to be named Jesus, generally thought to mean "God saves." However, Matthew says that this announcement was in direct fulfillment of Isaiah 7:14, which he quotes, "Look, the virgin shall conceive and bear a son, and they shall name him Emmanuel," and interprets, "which means 'God is with us'" (Matt 1:23). So, from the perspective of the New Testament, the historical Jesus is the fulfillment of the promise made by Isaiah many generations prior to the announcement to Joseph. The Incarnation is the assurance that God is always present for those who seek that eternal presence. For the Christian undergoing a period of personal crisis, the reason for the suffering may not be immediately apparent, but the certainty to which one can cling is that God is there in the midst of the suffering.

The return of the exiles reveals a difficult truth for those who may be estranged from God and are seeking a way back. The returning exiles hoped for immediate success in the land of promise, but as was discussed in session 8, *an easy path to restoration is seldom offered.* They faced the realities of foreigners in the land, the vagaries of the weather, corrupt officials, and many other hardships. Some were of their own making, caused by focusing on their own problems instead of rebuilding the temple. Others were simply the result of having been away for so long. Regardless of the reason, the path back required hard work and intense faith. Unfortunately, the book of Isaiah closes without evidence that the journey down that road was ever completed.

When ministers, pastoral counselors, or Christian friends talk to people who have rebelled against God, engaged in foolish or destructive behavior, and finally reached the point where they realize their only hope is a return to faith, these Christian servants often find that the person is eager to have the relationship restored. They are glad for the news that God desires their return and a renewal of an intimate connection. However, while forgiveness may be instantaneous, the road to spiritual, emotional, and physical health may be long and arduous. While some desire forgiveness, they may be unwilling to give up a particular sin, to engage in the battle necessary to overcome an addiction, or to offer apologies and restitution to those who have been hurt. God offers both forgiveness and the assurance of ongoing strength for the battles that may lie ahead, but there is no promise of peace without struggle.

An Example to Follow

We know very little about the personal life of the prophet Isaiah who was the central human character in the first thirty-nine chapters of the book that bears his name. We know virtually nothing about the subsequent prophets who proclaimed the word of God in the second and third sections of the book. Nevertheless, all of these prophets provide stirring examples of individuals willing to be used to proclaim the truth of God to people who were often resistant to the message, but who needed to hear it nonetheless.

Our tendency may be to think of these men from the distant past as eccentric characters, fulfilling a unique role as spokespersons for God. We have difficulty imagining ourselves receiving a call through a heavenly vision, or naming our children in such a way that they reveal the word of God to a nation. We certainly cannot see ourselves walking around naked for three years as the First Isaiah did in order to make a point to the king. It is hard to envision offering a word of comfort to large groups of exiles with any credibility. We are reluctant to preach to people about the need to refocus their priorities, to worship sincerely, or to take care of the less fortunate. John the Baptist may have been a prophet; so were latter-day figures like Dietrich Bonhoeffer and Martin Luther King, Jr., but not us. We'll leave prophecy to the preachers. If we do any preaching, it will have to be by the examples we set by the way we live.

The reality, however, is that the prophetic role is not limited to any age or to those who are singularly called for that purpose. The factor that all of the prophets of Isaiah as well as Elijah, Elisha, Jeremiah, Ezekiel, and all the rest had in common was that they were called by God to speak the truth to people who needed to hear it. Sometimes it was to people in power, but just as often it was to ordinary individuals who were on a dangerous path and needed to be warned about the consequences.

Writing in a time of severe persecution of Christians, Peter urged, "Always be ready to make your defense to anyone who demands from you an account of the hope that is in you" (1 Pet 3:15b). Many Christians today tend to practice their religion so privately that it is unlikely that anyone will ever demand an account. However, if we are involved in the life of the world, there will still be opportunities not only to defend our position as Christians but also to challenge others to live by God's standards. This includes exhorting other Christians, fellow members of the new covenant, to seek to please God. But it may also include speaking to the powers-that-be regarding the treatment of the last, the lost, and the least. The prophets understood that God had particular concern for the less fortunate and that we have a shared responsibility not only to treat them ethically but also to challenge others to do the same.

Prelude to the New Testament

The stirring oratorio *Messiah*, by G. F. Handel, has become one of the most beloved pieces of classical music. The Christmas portion of this work is familiar to people around the world, whether or not they are Christians. The *Hallelujah* chorus is one of the most recognizable compositions ever created. This is a decidedly Christian piece. It is a musical account of the Incarnation as experienced through the historical figure of Jesus of Nazareth. Yet it begins with a tenor singing the words of Second Isaiah: "Comfort ye, comfort ye my people, saith your God. Speak ye comfortably to Jerusalem, and cry unto her, that her warfare is accomplished, that her iniquity is pardoned. The voice of him that crieth in the wilderness; prepare ye the way of the LORD; make straight in the desert a highway for our God." Much of the remainder of the oratorio is a direct musical rendering of the prophecies of Isaiah (as well as other Old Testament prophets) and portions of the New Testament Book of Revelation. They are used as narrative for the events in the life of Jesus.

The *Messiah* may be one of the most dramatic indications of the connection in the minds of Christians between the book of Isaiah and the New Testament story of Jesus Christ. Many Christians assume that any reference in Isaiah to oracles that were *fulfilled* by Jesus were *intended* to be about Jesus. This does not have to be the case, however, for the connection between Isaiah and Jesus the Messiah to be valid.

According to the Gospel of Luke (4:16-19), when Jesus inaugurated his ministry in Galilee, he preached in his home synagogue in Nazareth. He read from the scroll of Isaiah verses that have come down to us as Isaiah 61:1 and 58:6, passages that speak about one on whom God's spirit rests, who had been given the specific message of bringing good news to the poor, liberty to the captives, recovery of sight to the blind, and freedom for the oppressed, and who was to announce that the time of salvation had arrived. Then he boldly declared, "This passage of scripture has come true today, as you heard it being read" (Luke 4:21). As Luke interprets the life of Jesus, it is a direct fulfillment of Isaiah regarding one who would come to deliver the people of the covenant.

At that point, according to Luke, many were impressed by his eloquence but some were skeptical about any claim by someone they knew personally, "the son of Joseph." However, they did not become enraged until Jesus cited two examples from the past of how God had been at work in the world. One was when Elijah was sent to live with a widow in Zarephath. The other was when Elisha healed Naaman the Syrian. What made them so furious that they wanted to kill Jesus was that both of these were examples of God working among Gentiles. They were to the point of throwing him off the edge of a cliff when he somehow walked through the middle of the crowd and made his way out of town.

This single incident, recorded in different form in Matthew 4, illustrates the connection that Jesus made between himself and the messianic expectations of Isaiah. Rather than fulfilling the hopes of the Jews for a reestablishment of the Jewish state in Judea, with a capital in Jerusalem, Jesus saw his role as something completely different. His reference to God working among the Gentiles pointed to his understanding of the people of the covenant being "a light to the nations" (Isa 49:6). His self-sacrificial death aptly fulfills the prophecy of Isaiah 53:

> Who has believed what we have heard? And to whom has the arm of the LORD been revealed? For he grew up before him like a young plant, and like a root out of dry ground; he had no form or majesty that we should look at him, nothing in his appearance that we should desire him. He was despised and rejected by others; a man of suffering and acquainted with infirmity; and as one from whom others hide their faces he was despised, and we held him of no account. Surely he has borne our infirmities and carried our diseases; yet we accounted him stricken, struck down by God, and afflicted. But he was wounded for our transgressions, crushed for our iniquities; upon him was the punishment that made us whole, and by his bruises we are healed. All we like sheep have gone astray; we have all turned to our own way, and the LORD has laid on him the iniquity of us all. (Isa 53:1-6)

There is probably no single passage in all the New Testament that more eloquently and accurately describes the mission and ministry of Jesus than this oracle composed centuries before his birth. The book of Isaiah is used more frequently by the writers of the New Testament than any other Hebrew Scripture other than the book of Psalms. The book contains so much that has been interpreted in relation to Jesus, either within the New Testament or by later writers, that it has come to be known as "the fifth Gospel." (One of the most comprehensive treatments of this subject is John F. A. Sawyer's *The Fifth Gospel: Isaiah in the History of Christianity*.)

Many New Testament scholars have addressed the individual citations of Isaiah, from the understanding of John the Baptist to the role of Jesus as the Suffering Servant to the purpose of the children of Judah, as applying to Jesus' mission to the Gentiles. For a full appreciation of this connection, consult the commentaries on books of the New Testament. However, as prelude to that study, begin with an understanding of the book of Isaiah in its historical context. This will add a depth and richness to one's understanding of Jesus as the Messiah that cannot be attained in any other way.

1. If someone were to ask you what the book of Isaiah is about, how would you respond?

_____
_____
_____
_____
_____

2. What do you see as the major theme of each of the three sections of the book? What do you think they have in common?

_____
_____
_____
_____
_____

3. What lessons have you learned from your study of Isaiah that you would add to the ones included in the section "A Cautionary Tale" in this chapter?

_____

_____

_____

_____

_____

4. What are some of the injustices against which a prophetic voice needs to be raised today?

_____

_____

_____

_____

_____

5. Why are modern Christians hesitant to speak out against issues our society faces?

_____

_____

_____

_____

_____

6. Think about your own expectations of what God will do for you. How are those ideas challenged by the role that Jesus chose as the Messiah?

_____

_____

_____

_____

_____

7. What questions did this study raise about Isaiah that were not answered? How will you continue to study Isaiah?

_____

_____

_____

_____

_____

Bibliography

Brooks, Phillips. *Lectures on Preaching*. London: H. R. Allenson, Ltd., 1877.

Brueggemann, Walter. *Isaiah 1–39* and *Isaiah 40–66* in *Westminster Bible Companion*. Patrick D. Miller and David L. Bartlett, Series Editors. Louisville: John Knox Press, 1998.

Buechner, Frederick. *Telling the Truth: The Gospel as Tragedy, Comedy and Fairy Tale*. San Francisco: Harper San Francisco, 1977.

Cate, Robert L. *Old Testament Roots for New Testament Faith*. Nashville: Broadman Press, 1982.

Childs, Brevard S. *Isaiah* in *The Old Testament Library*. James L. Mays et al., Advisory Board. Louisville: Westminster John Knox Press, 2001.

Conrad, Edgar W. "The 'Fear Not' Oracles in Second Isaiah," *Vestus Testamentum* 34/2 (1984): 129–52.

Hanson, Paul D. *Isaiah 40-66* in *Interpretation: A Bible Commentary for Teaching and Preaching*. James Luther Mays, Series Editor. Louisville: John Knox Press, 1995.

Harner, Philip B. "The Salvation Oracle in Second Isaiah." *Journal of Biblical Literature* 88/4 (December 1969): 418–34.

Kelley, Page H. *Isaiah*, vol. 5 in *The Broadman Bible Commentary*. Clifton J. Allen, General Editor. Nashville: Broadman Press, 1971.

Muilenburg, James and Henry Sloan Coffin. *The Book of Isaiah, Chapters 40-66*, vol. 5 in *The Interpreter's Bible*. George Arthur Buttrick, Commentary Editor. Nashville: Abingdon Press, 1952.

von Rad, Gerhard. *The Message of the Prophets.* New York: Oliver & Boyd Ltd, 1965.

Sawyer, John F. A. *The Fifth Gospel: Isaiah in the History of Christianity.* Cambridge: Cambridge University Press, 1996.

Scott, R. B. Y., and G. G. D. Kilpatrick. *The Book of Isaiah, Chapters 1-39,* vol. 5 in *The Interpreter's Bible.* George Arthur Buttrick, Commentary Editor. Nashville: Abingdon Press, 1952.

Seitz, Christopher R. *Isaiah 1-39* in *Interpretation: A Bible Commentary for Teaching and Preaching.* James Luther Mays, Series Editor. Louisville: John Knox Press, 1993.

Watts, John D. W. *Isaiah* in *Mercer Commentary on the Bible.* Watson E. Mills and Richard F. Wilson, General Editors. Macon GA: Mercer University Press, 1995.

Study the Bible...

Sessions Series

a book at a time

Series Editor:
Michael D. McCullar

The *Sessions* Series is our expanding set of Bible studies designed to encourage a deeper encounter with Scripture. Each volume includes eight to ten lessons as well as resource pages to facilitate preparation, class discussion, or individual Bible study.

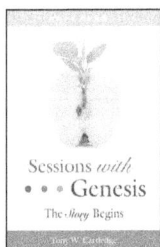

**Sessions
with Genesis**
The Story Begins
by Tony W. Cartledge

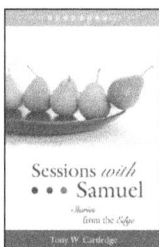

**Sessions
with Samuel**
Stories from the Edge
by Tony W. Cartledge

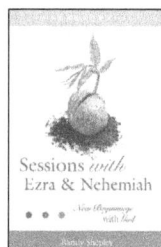

**Sessions
with Ezra &
Nehemiah**
New Beginnings with God
by Randy Shepley

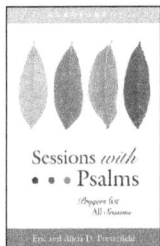

**Sessions
with Psalms**
Prayers for All Seasons
*by Eric and Alicia D.
Porterfield*

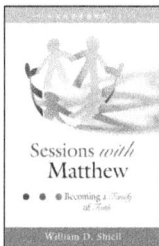

**Sessions
with Matthew**
Becoming a Family of Faith
by William D. Shiell

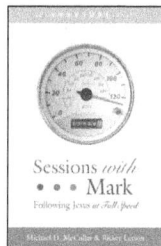

**Sessions
with Mark**
Following Jesus at Full Speed
*by Michael D. McCullar
& Rickey Letson*

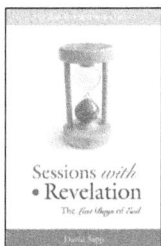

www.ingramcontent.com/pod-product-compliance
Lightning Source LLC
LaVergne TN
LVHW021517080426
835509LV00018B/2541